Praise for Lexa Roséan and Her Work

"Thanks to a few good witches out there, anyone can practice a little love magic these days. You don't even have to buy a cauldron. No eye of newt in the house? Not to worry. You need go no further than your fridge for the makings of many love spells, says Lexa Roséan. . . ."

—*Montreal Hour*

"Roséan, an astrologer and psychic who lives in New York, has written five books about witchcraft—a cheerful, positive witchcraft devoid of the stereotypical brooms, warts, and Satanic ritual."

—*The Miami Herald*

"Roséan's writing is spellbinding, as she tosses in funny anecdotes, folklore, and mythology. . . ."

—*The Advocate*

"Ms. Roséan has her share of satisfied customers. . . ."

—*The New York Times*

"Wisdom and more is packed into her book. . . ."

—*The Toronto Star*

"Roséan's spells [have] worked wonders for me. . . ."

—*Newsday*

"Her books contain spells and hexes for the modern urban Dorothy who wants to find her way home, or at least to a better apartment."

—*Jewish Week*

Other Books by Lexa Roséan

The Encyclopedia of Magickal Ingredients

A Wiccan Guide to Spellcasting

Lexa Roséan

Photos by Enrique Urrutia

Paraview Pocket Books

New York   London   Toronto   Sydney

PARAVIEW
191 Seventh Avenue, New York, NY 10011

POCKET BOOKS, a division of Simon & Schuster, Inc.
1230 Avenue of the Americas, New York, NY 10020

Library of Congress Cataloging-in-Publication Data

Roséan, Lexa.
    The encyclopedia of magickal ingredients: a wiccan guide to
    spellcasting / Lexa Roséan.—1st Paraview Pocket Books trade pbk. ed.
        p. cm.
    Includes bibliographical references.
    1. Magic—Encyclopedias. 2. Witchcraft—Encyclopedias.
    3. Charms—Encyclopedias. I. Title.

BF1611.R65 2005
133.4'4—dc22

                                                          2005050910

ISBN-13: 978-1-4165-0158-9
ISBN-10:   1-4165-0158-4

First Paraview Pocket Books trade paperback edition October 2005

 20 19 18 17 16 15

POCKET and colophon are registered trademarks of
Simon & Schuster, Inc.

Manufactured in the United States of America

Designed by Jaime Putorti

For information regarding special discounts for bulk purchases,
please contact Simon & Schuster Special Sales at 1-800-456-6798
or business@simonandschuster.com.

Warning

Do not use any ingredient in this book if you are allergic to it.

Disclaimer

One of the country's oldest occult shops is located on Philadelphia's South Street. A sign above the door reads: "All Items Sold As Curios Only." The owners have posted this sign to protect witches from those of little faith. The believers smile past the sign and buy the tools of their craft with perfect love and perfect trust.

The same disclaimer is issued for this book: "All ingredients and spells are provided as curios only." The information found in these pages merely serves to help you channel your will. Remember, the real magick is within you.

Turk Haremime: Yesim, Örgü, Elif

Contents

$\mathcal{E}$ 95

East • Echinacea • Egg • Eggplant • Elder • Elecampane • Elemental • Elements • Elephant • Elm • Emerald • Endive • Eucalyptus • Evening Primrose • Eyebright • Eye of Newt • Eyes

$\mathcal{F}$ 103

Feather • Fennel • Fenugreek • Fern • Feverfew • Fig • Fir Balsam • Fire • Fish • Five-Finger Grass • Flax • Floor Wash • Flour • Fluorite • Flying • Foxglove • Frangipani • Frankincense • Freesia • Friday

$\mathcal{G}$ 112

Galangal • Galbanum • Gardenia • Garlic • Garnet • Garter • Geranium • Ginger • Ginkgo • Ginseng • Glitter • Gnocchi • God • Goddess • Gold • Goldenseal • Gotu Kola • Gourd • Grains of Paradise • Grapefruit • Grapes • Green • Guarana • Guava

$\mathcal{H}$ 122

Hail • Hair • Hand • Harpie • Hawthorn • Hazel • Heal-All • Heart • Hearts of Palm • Heather • Heliotrope • Hellebore • Hematite • Hemlock • Hemp • Henbane • Henna • Herring • Hexagram • Hibiscus • Hickory • Holly • Honey • Honeydew • Honeysuckle • Hood • Hops • Horehound • Horseradish • Horseshoe • Horsetail • Huckleberry • Hyacinth • Hydrangea • Hyssop

Moldavite • Monday • Moonstone • Morning Glory • Moss • Mouth • Muguet • Mugwort • Mulberry • Mullein • Mushroom • Musk • Mustard • Myrrh • Myrtle

$\mathcal{N}$ 186

Nails, Finger- and Toe- • Nails, Iron • Naked • Names • Narcissus • Neptune • Neroli • Nettle • Newsprint • Nightshade • Nosegay • Numbers • Nutmeg • Nuts

O 194

Oak • Oak Moss • Oat • Oath • Obsidian • Oil • Ointments • Oleander • Olibanum • Olive • Onion • Onyx • Opal • Opium • Orange • Orchid • Oregano • Orris • Owl • Oysters

$\mathcal{P}$ 203

Paella • Palm • Palmarosa • Pancakes • Pansy • Papaya • Paprika • Papyrus • Parchment • Parsley • Parsnip • Passionflower • Passion Fruit • Pasta • Patchouli • Pea • Peach • Pear • Pearl • Pennies • Pennyroyal • Pentagram • Peony • Pepper, Spice • Pepper, Vegetable • Peppermint • Perfume • Peridot • Periwinkle • Persimmon • Pesto • Petitgrain • Petrified Wood • Peyote • Pickle • Picture • Pie • Pierogi • Pillow • Pimiento • Pine • Pineapple • Pink • Pins • Pizza • Plantain • Plum • Poke • Pomegranate • Poplar • Poppet • Poppy • Potato • Pretzel • Prune • Pumpkin • Purple • Purselane

The
Encyclopedia
of Magickal
Ingredients

Introduction

The Encyclopedia of Magickal Ingredients is a quick and easy guide to help you locate the items you need to create spells tailored to your specific needs and desires. You can also use this guide to understand why you find yourself craving, or are for some reason attracted to certain scents, flavors, or foods. Just as the body can tell us what it needs, so can the soul.

Take oranges, for example. Scientists tell us that oranges contain vitamin C. Legend tells us that Jove gave the orange blossom to the goddess Juno on their wedding day and therefore both the blossom and the fruit of the orange contain vibrations of true love. So in the same way that the body craves oranges because it needs vitamin C, the spiritual body may be craving oranges because it needs a soul mate.

Everything under the sun (and moon) has a magickal property and astrological assignment, an affinity with a certain god or goddess, and/or a spiritual vibration. From ancient times to modern day, occultists and spiritual practitioners continue the work of classifying ingredients and categorizing them by their spiritual attributes.

In this book you will find that each ingredient is assigned an astrological or god/goddess *ruler,* a *type* to help you identify it, and a *magickal form* describing the best way to use the product. The entries explain the magickal properties and associations of each item, plus provide an easy spell to accomplish a desired goal. This presentation not only enables the beginner to create simple spells with a single ingredient, but it allows the advanced practitioner to create personalized spells using a blend of ingredients.

What Is a Spell?

A spell can be as simple as a prayer. It can be a food that is eaten with a wish or visualization for something special to manifest. It can be an elaborate ritual perfectly timed with chants and bells, dancing and libations.

Spells work on many levels. As prayers, they often involve offering petitions or gifts to gods or goddesses in exchange for the fulfillment of your request. For petition spells, it is important to know what the gods and goddesses prefer. The *Ruler* category under each ingredient will help you determine this preference.

The ingredients used in spells hold particular powers or properties, and by ingesting them, rubbing them on our skin, smelling them when they are burned, or surrounding ourselves with them, we will gain these qualities in our lives. Like vitamins, these ingredients will be absorbed into our spiritual and physical bodies and bring us benefit.

Ritual, or spellwork, also works beyond the physical level. Spells are also symbolic, and the ingredients act as keys to unlock unconscious potential. They serve as vehicles to focus and drive the will. Whether it is through prayer, properties, or potential, spells are known to work and bring manifestation of desires.

A spell can be worked as often as you would say a prayer. Repetition is very powerful in bringing about magickal manifestation, although you may not want to "bug" the gods and goddesses with too many requests. My suggestion is to focus on one magickal issue at a time for an entire waxing or waning moon phase. (See moon phases section in this introduction for an explanation.) You will find that this brings the best results.

Personalized Spells

Why is this encyclopedia of magickal ingredients better than a traditional spellbook? Because you can use it to create spells that are personalized to your own circumstance and need. For example, traditional money spells often call for roots, which are very powerful. But root ingredients are used to literally "root" finances. Roots are great if you are starting a business and want to make sure the foundation is strong. Roots also work quite well for saving money over a long period of time, but they're not going to manifest the rent money by next Tuesday! For that you need fiery fast-luck ingredients.

For drawing large sums in money magick, I recommend Jupiterian and solar ingredients. But be careful! Jupiter makes more of whatever is already there, and if you've got nothing— well, Jupiter magick will give you more of nothing, or even worse, double your debt. Ouch! Ingredients ruled by the

Moon, Mercury, Mars, and Venus work quickly and are more likely to stir up finances from scratch. So with this guide you can personalize your spells and target exactly how you wish to succeed.

Most spellbooks do not explain why you should use the ingredients they recommend or what their magickal properties are. In 1996, with the publication of my book *The Supermarket Sorceress*, I began explaining the properties of the ingredients along with the directions for working the spells. Since that time, I have received thousands of inquiries for personalized spells. The idea for this book arose from those requests.

It is almost impossible to write one spell to cover each individual's needs. This book will help you customize your spells for your specific desires. It will provide you with the confidence you need to prepare your own spell blends.

Let's take a look at a generic love spell, for example. It might consist of red peppers for passion, tomatoes for nurturing, and basil for communication. The fourth ingredient is garlic, which brings fertility. But maybe you're not ready for kids just yet! With this book, you will be able to design your own love spell to attract only the qualities you want.

You will also find this book quite handy for understanding the ingredients listed in other spellbooks. In the same way that you read nutritional information about food, or the side effects of drugs, you will want to be familiar with all the properties of your magickal ingredients.

Locating the Ingredients

The number-one issue that comes up with my clients and readers is their inability to find ingredients called for in spells.

The reality is that when the moon is full and the time is ripe for doing magick, you will not always have on hand the items you need.

Fear not. This book will enable you to find substitutes. A desperate woman in Iowa who couldn't find corn for her prosperity spell contacted me. If you can't find corn in the Corn Belt, I don't know where you can find it! But lucky for the lady in Des Moines, she had some oatmeal in her cupboard. It made a fine substitute.

And what about all those ingredients you do have handy, but have no idea what their purpose might be? This book will tell you how they can be used. And I cover quite a range of ingredients. This book describes food products as well as herbs, oils, flowers, common household items, and traditional witches' tools. Some are for internal use, others are not. I am often asked which type of spell is better—one that works with food (or kitchen witchery) or a spell that is more traditional (like burning incense and candles). This depends on the nature of the situation.

Again, let's take a money spell, for example. Internal magick, which involves ingesting something, will create inner drive. This is particularly good for people who have the external opportunities but don't have the motivation to respond and take advantage of them. So in this case, eating prosperity foods would be the best spell. Another person, however, may have plenty of drive but no external opportunity. In this case, a spell using something outside of oneself will create possibilities in the outer world to meet the individual's ambitions. In some cases, both types are beneficial. That's why I include *all* types of magickal ingredients in this book.

Too Many Choices

Another frequently asked question is why there are so many ingredients for love, or wealth, or success, for example. Which one should I use? The answer to this question is simple. Spell ingredients are much like pharmaceuticals. They are magickal prescriptions, if you will. Not everyone responds well to the same medicine. You will have to experiment until you find the one that works best for you. The best way to make the right choice is to use what you are attracted to. Trust your intuition.

At the end of this book you will find the Magickal Tables, a quick and easy reference guide to spell topics. Under each topic you will find a list of ingredients that correspond to that kind of magick. For example, under the Magickal Money Table you will find a list of all ingredients that can be used in money spells. You can then look up the related entries and learn about the properties of each individual item. These tables will make it easier for you to find the right ingredients when you know what kind of spell you want to perform.

Forms, Methods, and Timing

The ingredients used in spells take different forms, there are several methods to activate them, and releasing their energies involves proper timing. Here is a little guide to the terminology used in this book.

Altars are tables that are set up for general or specific purposes. An all-purpose altar contains an image of a god and goddess and a representation of each of the four elements: a bowl of salt (earth), a bowl of water (water), an incense burner and incense (air), and a candle (fire). The altar can serve a specific purpose—for love, healing, success, or protection, for example—by adding images and ingredients that relate to these themes.

Baths are an essential practice in magick. A magickal bath is best taken on a new or full moon. Once ingredients are added to the bathwater, the practitioner should soak for a minimum of ten minutes. You should already be clean before taking a magickal bath. After the soak, you should not soap or rinse off for twenty-four hours. Baths represent both water and earth so they affect both the emotions and the physical body.

Candles are burned to make magickal requests. The candles can be carved with seals or requests written upon their surface. The candles are then rubbed with oils or powdered herbs that are associated with the magickal request. It is also common to surround the burning candle with a circle of herbs or flowers. Candles represent the element of fire, which makes them the most powerful magickal tool to influence actions.

Incense is available in sticks, cones, or loose incense made with herbs and essential oils and burned on charcoal briquettes in a cast-iron pot or cauldron. Incense represents the element of air, which makes it the most powerful magick to influence thought.

Oils are used for anointing the body or candles or metal and paper talismans. Oil can be a pure extract or a blend of several scents to create a certain magickal effect. Oil represents the elements of water, which means it is the most powerful form of magick to influence the emotions.

Offerings are left as prayers for specific deities. Some offerings are left on altars until prayers are answered. Others are brought to places such as rivers, oceans, or underneath trees and left for gods or goddesses. Offerings are representative of the earth element (no matter what the offering is), so they are the best magick to bring about physical manifestation.

Ouanga bags are cloth bags with drawstrings that are stuffed with herbs, roots, drops of oil, or other magickal ingredients. They are then carried or worn as talismans. After filling the bag with the ingredients, you must activate the ouanga by adding the four elements. First strike a match (fire) and throw it into the bag. Then immediately blow the match out (air), and spit (water) into the bag. Pull the drawstring tight and seal the bag with seven knots. The fourth element (earth) is represented by the contents of the bag (herbs, flowers, roots, etc.).

Moon cycles are important to the timing of your spells. Most Wiccans work closely with them. There are two moon cycles. The *waxing* cycle occurs for fourteen days beginning on the new moon and ending on the full moon. Because the moon grows larger during this time, this is the cycle of increase. Do magick to draw positive things into your life. The *waning* cycle occurs for fourteen days beginning on the full moon and ending on the new moon. Because the moon grows smaller during this time, this is the cycle of decrease. Do magick to rid yourself of negative situations.

Moon phases are also crucial to the timing of spells. There are three moon phases. The maiden is the *new moon*. This is the best time to begin a new project or do magick for something new you want to create in your life. The mother is the *full moon*. This is the best time to raise full power toward an aspect of your life that is already in the works. It is the time to bring something to its full potential. The crone is the *dark moon* and occurs one day before the new moon. At this time there is no visible light emanating from the lunar orb. This is a time for reflection, wisdom, or to diminish or end something. To find out where the moon is grab a good astrological ephemeris (I recommend Jim Maynard's *Celestial Guide*). You can also find this information in the weather section of your local newspaper.

Wishing you good luck and good magick.

Blessed be,
Lexa Roséan
aka Lady Venus ☆

A

Acacia

RULER: Zeus, Obatala, Ra, Bast, solar deities
TYPE: plant
MAGICKAL FORM: oil, bark, branch, flower

Sitting under an acacia tree or burning the dried flowers brings wisdom and insight. The oil extracted from the plant is considered holy and used for purification and anointing. It is especially powerful when attempting to contact the dead and should be rubbed into white candles and not worn on the body while attempting such work. For personal anointing, mix with other oils (like musk or camellia) to cut and then it is said to bring happiness.

Acorn

RULER: Jupiter
TYPE: tree nut
MAGICKAL FORM: dried

Wisdom and prosperity are the main properties of the acorn. It is a symbol of great luck and fortune. Witches gather acorns and add them to autumn equinox altars to invoke nurturing and safekeeping during the coming winter months. On a full moon or a Thursday during a waxing moon, wrap a dollar bill over an acorn. Make sure the pyramid symbol of the dollar bill is facing outside. Then carry the dollar bill in your wallet to attract money and help you to handle your finances wisely.

Adam and Eve Roots

RULER: Venus
TYPE: plant
MAGICKAL FORM: root

The round root is Eve and the oblong root is Adam. Bind these two roots together with red string and place them on a love altar or sew them up in a red cloth bag and carry as a talisman for love attraction. Gay males will want two Adams and lesbians will want two Eves. Carry to conjure a new love or to keep an ongoing relationship happy. Rub the bodily fluids of each member of a couple into his/her respective root to prevent cheating and ensure fidelity in the relationship.

Agate

RULER: Venus
TYPE: mineral
MAGICKAL FORM: various colors

An emotional healing stone, the agate is carried to summon courage. Wear *blue* agate for protection. Carry *pink* agate to solve love problems. *Green* agate brings good luck and prosperity. Hold the stone between your hands to improve the balance and create more harmony in your life. The agate, along with most gemstones, is used in healing rites.

Air

RULER: east
TYPE: element
MAGICKAL FORM: incense, wind

Each of the four directions is ruled by an element. The east is associated with air and represents thought and imagination. All burning of incense is an invocation to the spirits of air. Wind is also used in ritual to carry or receive messages. This is done by shouting wishes or requests into a strong wind or releasing requests written on small squares of parchment paper into an eastern wind.

Alfalfa

RULER: Venus
TYPE: herb
MAGICKAL FORM: seeds, sprouts

Eat alfalfa sprouts to increase your income. It is especially helpful in obtaining loans or monies owed you. Sprinkle the seeds in prosperity rituals during waxing moons and keep some in kitchens during waning moons to ward off poverty. Eat alfalfa on Fridays for love.

Allspice

RULER: Jupiter
TYPE: spice
MAGICKAL FORM: whole berries, powder

Add this all-around winning ingredient to any success formula to increase chances of beating out the competition. Carry the whole berries in the pocket to improve your chances on interviews or winning clients. Sprinkle the powder across a place of business or dust the hands when you want to succeed. Allspice is especially effective when cooked in water in a double boiler to fill a room with its scent. Doing so opens the brain centers to greater achievement and creates a happy, efficient work environment.

Aloe

RULER: Moon
TYPE: plant
MAGICKAL FORM: juice, leaf

Keeping an aloe plant is said to ward off evil and accidents. Of course, when accidents do occur, it is a very handy plant to have around the house. The healing properties of the aloe are legendary. Open the leaves and apply to cuts and burns. The cooling effects drive away hot energy and can also calm down angry and heated emotions. When dried and hung above the doorway, aloe drives away evil. Ingest aloe juice for health and longevity. Rub into the body on a full moon for sexual stamina and allure.

Altar

RULER: various
TYPE: various
MAGICKAL FORM: focal point for magick

Witches set up altars before casting their magick circles. A *traditional* altar holds representations of the four elements: cauldron of incense (air), red candle (fire), bowl of water (water), bowl of salt (earth). God and goddess statues are placed in the center surrounded by seasonal flowers, a black candle, and a white candle. Needed also are a pentacle for blessing food and a libation bowl for offerings. This is the most basic setup, although altars become more elaborate for specific ceremonies. *Ceremonial* altars can be quite elaborate with specific requirements for type of wood, measurements, and shape. *Improvisational* altars can be created on a shelf, nightstand, or table. Use any magickal images that inspire you. *Money* or *success* altars should include coins and grain offerings. *Love* altars can include pictures of loved ones, red, pink, or white flowers, and honey or sugar cubes. *Healing* altars should have crystals, yellow and white candles, and any images you associate with healing or a photograph of the person who needs healing. The altar can be a permanent fixture or resting place for a deity you worship or a temporary structure that is dismantled once a ritual has been completed and the magickal energy has been raised.

Amazonite

RULER: Moon, Diana
TYPE: mineral
MAGICKAL FORM: rounded stone

A stone of female power and intuitiveness, this green stone is similar to jade. Unlike jade, which is said to be fickle, Amazonite is the stone of truth. When carried, it improves your character and self-esteem. Hold the stone up to the light of a full moon to charge and then place on an altar or table during divination. It will increase your clairvoyant ability and bring more clarity to your psychic work. The stone is also the best choice to use for emotional healings for women or for men to bring forth the positive aspect of their feminine sides.

Amber

RULER: Sun
TYPE: mineral
MAGICKAL FORM: resin, gemstone, essential oil

This golden gemstone is a favorite among witches and is beaded together in a necklace with jet. This special necklace symbolizes the power of the goddess and is worn only by the high priestess of the coven. Wear or carry amber for protection and success. A stone that contains a beetle or fly trapped within its center is said to bring fame. Add the resin to prosperity formulas and wear the oil for protection or to empower your magickal path. Men may wear this oil to attract lovers.

Ambergris

RULER: Venus, Neptune
TYPE: animal extract
MAGICKAL FORM: real or synthetic oil

This prized oil is derived from the sperm whale and most difficult to obtain, but there are some good chemical compound substitutes. Use ambergris for love, sex, lust, and, believe it or not, spiritual elevation. This makes it one of the best oils for tantric sex. Rub on red yoni and phallus candles, mix the oil with musk crystals to stir passions, or wear the oil on pulse points to increase spiritual awareness and sexual attraction.

Amethyst

RULER: Jupiter, Neptune
TYPE: mineral
MAGICKAL FORM: raw cut crystal

This stone is more powerful when unpolished. It should be given to or carried by mourners to bring them comfort in their time of loss. Place the stone by the bedside of terminal patients to help them transition from this world into the next. Amethyst is also very useful in breaking a bad habit. The stone is especially effective in curing alcohol addiction. Soak in a tub with three of the gemstones and then carry one in your pocket to strengthen your resolve to stay away from negative influences. A carried stone also helps alleviate stress.

Ammonia

RULER: dark Moon
TYPE: chemical
MAGICKAL FORM: liquid

Always use ammonia in small amounts, as it is a baneful compound. Use it in cursing magic and also to remove hexes. A few drops added to the bathwater will remove the most stubborn of hexes. Scrub down floors and walls with ammonia diluted in water to remove evil spirits from a dwelling.

Anchovies

RULER: sea goddesses
TYPE: fish
MAGICKAL FORM: whole, paste

Legend holds that anchovies bond together to create the hair of mermaids. These tiny fish attract beauty and hold the power of seduction. Eat them or carry them in a tin to attract beautiful women or to make yourself more beautiful. Spread the paste with the thumb on a cracker and feed to another to seduce.

Angelica

RULER: Sun
TYPE: herb
MAGICKAL FORM: root

Burn the powdered root when you want to invoke angels. Angelica is a healing herb. Mix in bathwater to promote good health. It also removes hexes. Sprinkle around the house to ward off evil or dry dust the body to remove a curse. Angelica is also considered lucky, so rub the root between your palms when you gamble or pick your lottery numbers.

Angels

RULER: air
TYPE: ethereal beings
MAGICKAL FORM: signatures

Judeo-Christian and Islamic lore are full of angel magick. Ceremonial magick includes many rituals and invocations to summon their presence. The Enochian alphabet is the language of angels and sigils are drawn with these letters to invoke specific angels. The four archangels are invoked in the LBR (Lesser Banishing Ritual) for protection. Blending Wicca and ceremonial magick, these four angels are each assigned a quarter to guard: Raphael in the east, Gabriel in the west, Michael in the south, and Uriel in the north.

Anise

RULER: Jupiter
TYPE: herb
MAGICKAL FORM: seeds, root, extract

Chewing on *raw licorice root* curbs the appetite and is a great (and healthy) tool for weight loss. Rub the *oil* into red or white candles for weight-loss spells. Add *anise seed* to love formulas to curb the sexual appetites of a cheating lover. Combine with cumin and rub on male or female figure candles to keep a lover faithful. Use *licorice whips* to control and harness energy. Tie a knot in the whip as you say a few words about your issue (example: can't focus, need better grades, want a lover). Press your thumb and middle finger over the knot and repeat your issue three times and then eat the whip to focus and harness your energy. For love matters use red whips. For all other matters, use black ones.

Apache Tear

RULER: earth and warrior goddesses
TYPE: mineral
MAGICKAL FORM: polished drops or tears

Legend says these tears, a form of black obsidian and volcanic glass, were formed by Apache women crying over the loss of all the warriors who fought for their land. Use the stone to rectify karmic situations, especially those having to do with land ownership. Scatter a handful of the black tears over a property in ownership dispute. The rightful owner will achieve victory (without tears). Carry the stone for luck and to bring forgiveness and settle grievances between enemies.

Apple

RULER: Venus
TYPE: fruit
MAGICKAL FORM: whole, seed, stem, oil

The forbidden fruit yields much power. Cut it in half horizontal to the stem to reveal the sacred witches' pentagram. Apples are a food of love. Offer a bite to a prospective lover. If he or she accepts, you will begin a love affair. Twist the stem of an apple while calling out the letters of the alphabet. The letter you call out as the stem breaks will be the first letter of the name of your true love. Rub apple oil or fragrance on red candles to bring true love. Leave an offering of an apple under a tree for Venus and make a request for love. *Red apples* are for love, *golden apples* for fame and popularity, and *green apples* for prosperity.

Apricot

RULER: Sun
TYPE: fruit
MAGICKAL FORM: flesh, pit, dried, raw

Eat raw apricot for energy and rejuvenation. Consume the dried fruit to increase your life span. Dry the pits and add them to ouanga bags or poppets (voodoo dolls) for healing. The pit can also be ground to a powder and added to healing incense recipes. Finally, use the apricot in love spells to heal and reunite a couple whose relationship is on the rocks.

Aquamarine

RULER: Neptune
TYPE: mineral
MAGICKAL FORM: cut and polished

Carry this stone for protection when traveling on water or flying through the air over water. The blue of this stone influences the elements of both water (color of the ocean) and air (color of the sky). It is believed to prevent drowning and suffocating, bring inner peace, and reveal the mysteries of the deep. Meditation upon this stone can help open the creative unconscious. Carry or hold when inspiration is needed or to calm unreasonable fears. The stone should be cleansed with pure seawater to optimize its powers.

Arabic Gum

RULER: Mercury
TYPE: plant resin
MAGICKAL FORM: gum or powder

Add gum resin to loose incense formulas as a fixative and to raise spiritual consciousness. Burn or sprinkle the powder during rituals where requests or prayers are being made to deities. Arabic gum increases the chances of delivering messages and opens the psychic channels. It is also great for doing channeling work.

Arrowroot

RULER: Mars
TYPE: plant
MAGICKAL FORM: powder

Native Americans named this starch arrowroot because it was used to cure poison arrow wounds. Use in magickal recipes to heal a heart broken by one of Cupid's arrows. Sprinkle the powder in the four corners of a nursery to protect an infant. Dust your body to change your destiny, as arrowroot is said to avert Arachne, the weaver of fate.

Artichoke

RULER: Mars
TYPE: vegetable
MAGICKAL FORM: heart, leaves

As a member of the thistle family, artichokes carry armor and are eaten to ward off danger. Use them in rituals to get to the heart of a matter. Slowly work your way through the delicacy, peeling the leaves until you are at its core. Visualize the problem you are trying to sort out as you strip the leaves away. When you arrive at the heart, imagine your problem being solved at its very core. *Roman artichokes* stimulate the energy glands and increase sexual and physical stamina.

Arugula

RULER: Mars
TYPE: plant
MAGICKAL FORM: salad greens

The nutty peppery taste of arugula combined with its dark green color is said to bring cleverness in financial matters to those who consume it. Eat some on Tuesdays during a waxing moon to gain insight into your investments. The ancient Romans ate arugula as an aphrodisiac. Eat it with tomatoes to improve your sex life.

Asafoetida

RULER: Kali
TYPE: spice
MAGICKAL FORM: powder

This powerful-smelling spice is often used like garlic in East Indian cooking. It has protective powers much like garlic. Eat it to ward off evil. Sprinkle the powder around a property to protect it from thieves. Wearing asafoetida is said to cure homosexuality. Of course, the wearing of this scent will turn off just about everyone no matter what his or her sexual orientation.

Ash

RULER: Sun, Neptune
TYPE: plant
MAGICKAL FORM: leaves, bark, tree

In Medieval England and Ireland the ash tree was believed to repel snakes, remove warts, and protect children from witchcraft. Ancient Norse mythology describes the ash as the World Tree Yggdrassil. This tree is also sacred to sea gods. Carry the bark as a talisman when you are traveling across water. The ash tree is one of the sacred trees of the Druids and consecrating a branch of ash for use as a sacred wand will help to channel and reveal their ancient mysteries.

Ashes

RULER: fire, air
TYPE: mineral
MAGICKAL FORM: residue from something that is burned

The religious and magickal uses of ash include weather magic, healing, divination, acknowledgment of mortality and immortality, resurrection, mourning, purification, repentance, sorrow, protection, the conquering of fear, remembrance, fertility, and luck. Ash also represents the intellect, memory, new clarity, and vision. The best known spiritual rite using ash is the burning of the sacred palm to obtain ashes to mark the forehead on Ash Wednesday. Witches burn paper or herbal talismans to unlock their energy and work with the ash to bring about magickal transformation.

Asparagus

RULER: Zeus, Jupiter, Mars
TYPE: vegetable
MAGICKAL FORM: steamed

Eat this phallic vegetable for power, protection, prosperity, and sexual stamina. For best results, always consume the tops first and work your way down to the stem. In prosperity spells, it is best to work with a green dipping sauce that has a basil or cilantro base. For sex, use hollandaise or a white cream sauce. With a Parmesan or Romano cheese topping asparagus provides protection.

Aventurine

RULER: Jupiter
TYPE: mineral
MAGICKAL FORM: round

   Excitement and adventure are the two main vibrations of this gemstone. Hold and warm the stone between your hands while making a travel or dream vacation wish. Add this gem to money and job rituals to bring more success. Aventurine is also a healing stone used to calm the nerves and create balance in the physical body.

Avocado

RULER: Venus
TYPE: vegetable
MAGICKAL FORM: meat, skin, pit

   Many facial and anti-aging treatments contain avocado, which is a favorite beauty enhancer. Avocado softens and relaxes your skin when spread as a paste. Eat it for beauty and relaxation and serve it to calm down a potential lover and put him or her at ease. Dry the skin and crush it into a fine powder for adding to glamour incense formulas. Grow a plant from a pit to increase your physical attraction.

Azalea

RULER: Pluto, Persephone
TYPE: flower
MAGICKAL FORM: fresh

This flower is poisonous and has been used to commit suicide. It brings knowledge of the beyond and is a reminder of Persephone's departure into the underworld. Cut flowers placed on an altar will aid the emotional journey into the abyss and reveal knowledge of what lies behind death. Meditation on this flower growing in a garden connects us with the preciousness of life.

Azurite

RULER: Venus
TYPE: mineral
MAGICKAL FORM: deep blue clusters

Give this stone to someone you think is lying. It will encourage him or her to tell the truth. A great gem for honesty in love relationships and when meditated upon, it will help those involved see things from the other's perspective. Azurite is great to use when patience is required or when you are attempting to transform a relationship.

Bacon

RULER: Adonis
TYPE: meat
MAGICKAL FORM: cooked meat, grease, fat

The pig is considered unclean in Jewish and Muslim beliefs, but by most pagan accounts it is regarded as a symbol of prosperity. The pig or boar is the sacred totem animal of Adonis, the Greek god of vegetation and renewal who was sacrificed annually to ensure the fertility of the earth. The expression "bringing home the bacon" refers to making money; eat bacon to increase earnings. Smear the fat or grease on your body to remove marital tension and forgive adulterous affairs.

Bagel

RULER: Neptune
TYPE: bread
MAGICKAL FORM: various

Eat bagels to create illusions. The more you pile on top of the bagel, the more people will believe (and enjoy) the tall tales you tell. This is a great formula for fiction writers and political candidates. Never ever put ham (or any pork product) on a bagel. It brings very bad luck. Meditate on the *hole* in the bagel when you need to pull a quick disappearing act (especially from creditors). *Sesame bagels* are for prosperity. *Poppy bagels* eaten before bed increase dream activity. *Salt bagels* get rid of inconsistencies and make one a better liar. *Cinnamon raisin bagels* make flattery come easy. The *everything bagel* makes wishes come true.

Baking Soda

RULER: Moon
TYPE: chemical compound
MAGICKAL FORM: white powder

Use this compound for cleansing and to remove stubborn negative energy. It absorbs foul odors and foul entities. Add a scoop to bathwater or floor wash to cleanse a person or an area. Sprinkle some in a circle around the room and stand inside it for serious protection.

Balm of Gilead

RULER: Venus
TYPE: resin of plant
MAGICKAL FORM: essential oil, pod seed resin

Cleopatra procured King Herod's sacred groves of the balsam balm of Gilead and transferred the crops from Judea (the only place, it was alleged, they were able to grow) into Upper Egypt. The crops greatly improved the failing economy of her dynasty. A symbol of sacredness and prosperity, the balm of Gilead is also a favorite ingredient in true love blends. It opens the heart and increases sensual pleasure. Crush the pods into incense blends or dab the fragrant oil over the heart.

Bamboo

RULER: Buddha
TYPE: plant
MAGICKAL FORM: fresh shoots, dried wood

Live shoots growing in the home or garden bring luck and protection to the residents. Grow bamboo or keep some in water for prosperity and luck; be sure to place it in the western corner of a room. Reed pipes made of bamboo wood are played in magick circles to summon success and wealth. Place your fingers on the knots of a dried bamboo wand and make a wish. Boats are also made of bamboo wood, and floating a bamboo stick on a lake while making a wish is also believed to bring good luck and protection of an enterprise.

Banana

RULER: Mars
TYPE: fruit
MAGICKAL FORM: flesh, skin

Carry a banana in your travel bag and eat it during the journey to prevent harm and accidents while traveling on the road or in an airplane. Visualize a safe trip while you eat the fruit. Save the skin and give it as an offering to the earth after you have arrived safely at your destination. The skin or protective covering can also be dried and crushed into a powder; rub it into your body to increase sexual stamina.

Barley

RULER: Venus, Mercury
TYPE: grain
MAGICKAL FORM: raw, cooked

Eat these grains of prosperity on Wednesdays to increase earnings in creative or artistic endeavors. Barley is also eaten or sprinkled across altars for love and fertility on Fridays. On a full moon, throw raw seeds to the four quarters to bring money into an establishment.

Basil

RULER: Mars
TYPE: herb
MAGICKAL FORM: fresh, dried

A lust herb, basil's powerful aroma calls forth the sexual energy; eat it to invigorate the sexual appetite. Basil can also be burned to increase sensual pleasures. Place the dried leaves under a bed to reawaken the sex drive in a relationship. Eat basil on a Tuesday to summon physical strength or to prepare for battle. Consume on a Wednesday to open channels of communication.

Baths

RULER: water
TYPE: activity
MAGICKAL FORM: ritual bath

Magickal baths are different from ordinary baths. To begin with, the practitioner must be physically clean before immersion. The bathtub should be filled with warm water, then various salts, herbs, flowers, or oils are added to form the desired magickal recipe. Soak for ten minutes while visualizing your desire. It is believed that the magickal bath infuses the aura with properties and attributes that then influence your physical life. In Wiccan rites, the ritual bath is taken before casting a circle to cleanse and prepare the body for spiritual work.

Bay

RULER: Sun, Apollo
TYPE: herb
MAGICKAL FORM: leaves, powder, oil

An all-around successful herb, bay or bay laurel was originally offered only to the gods. Later on it was used to crown the victors of the ancient Olympic games. It is still considered an herb of success and victory. Add the leaves to bathwater or crush them into powder and burn it for success, or sprinkle it around a place of business to draw customers. Add oil to green candles for money spells. Cook bay leaves in soup for protection. When you find a bay leaf in your soup bowl, bite it between your teeth and make a wish. Bay is considered a dual-fold herb and can remove evil from a dwelling as well as bless it with positive energy.

Bayberry

RULER: Saturn
TYPE: herb
MAGICKAL FORM: oil, bark, root

Burn candles scented with bayberry oil in the home for protection and prosperity. Sprinkle powdered root on your money to attract more money and rub some into your wallet to protect it from theft.

Beans

RULER: Mercury
TYPE: vegetable
MAGICKAL FORM: raw, cooked

Use beans to appease the spirits of the dead. Throw some around the outside of the home if a ghost or poltergeist is bothering you. Beans inspire creativity and communication and can be carried raw in a pouch or cooked and eaten for inspiration. *Black turtles* help to jump hurdles and make important decisions. *Butter beans* reduce stress. *Canary beans* bring happiness and success in the arts. *Cow* or *black-eyed peas* bring luck and increase psychic vision. *Cranberry (October) beans* attract new opportunities. *Fava beans* bring power. *Garbanzos* (*chickpeas*) help beat the competition. *Great northern beans* bring discovery and insight; they also help to protect plans and keep them secret. *Green baby lima beans* bring new income. *Green splits* are for money or health. *Green pigeon beans* represent resourcefulness and money. *Large lima beans* allow expansion and financial growth. *Lentils* bring peace and financial security. *Navy beans* increase strength and determination. *Oval white beans* protect assets. *Pink beans* bring confidence and romance. *Pinto beans* open channels and create action and movement. *Red kidney beans* represent wisdom, love, and healing. *Roman beans* bring power and precision. *Small red beans* provide energy and lust. *Speckled lima beans* create networking opportunities. *Whole green beans* attract money and *yellow splits* bring luck and fame.

Bearberry

RULER: Diana
TYPE: plant
MAGICKAL FORM: dried herb

Native Americans add bearberry (scientific name *uva-ursi*) to medicine bags for vision quests. Sprinkle some around the altar before meditation. If children walk across this herb, they will be protected from abuse.

Bedsheets

RULER: Venus
TYPE: fabric
MAGICKAL FORM: sex stained

To keep a partner faithful or to get a lover to return to you, cut off a small corner of a bedsheet you have had sex together on. Glue it to the back of a picture of both of you and anoint the four corners of the photo with almond oil. Place under the bed and he or she will love only you or return to love you alone.

Beech

RULER: Mercury
TYPE: tree
MAGICKAL FORM: branch, bark

Use a beech branch as a wand to open channels for communication with the gods and spirits. It will enable you to quickly draw down divine energy into the circle. Carry small pieces of the bark in your pocket for luck and success. Place powder in right shoe to lead you toward your fortune.

Beer

RULER: Mars
TYPE: alcoholic beverage
MAGICKAL FORM: bath

The main ingredient used in beer is hops, which was used in biblical times for purification. Add a quart of beer to your bathwater to remove an evil eye or negative energy sent by someone jealous of you and who wants to cause you harm. Soak for ten minutes and immerse completely three times. When you leave the bath, wrap in a white towel or bathrobe and recite the Twenty-third psalm. Beer can also be consumed in small amounts (one glass or one bottle) to calm the nerves and protect you from harm.

Bees

RULER: Sophia
TYPE: insect
MAGICKAL FORM: live

The biblical land of milk and honey was partly a gift of the bees. They are considered sacred insects that bring both blessings (pollination/honey) and curses (stings). Bees are called the messengers of prayer and are sometimes referred to as angels. They are sacred to the Mother Goddess and represent her wisdom. Wherever they congregate, her mysteries lie. Beekeepers are considered sacred priests and priestesses of the occult secrets. When a bee is seen, one should ask it to impart some wisdom—but be careful not to get stung.

Beeswax

RULER: bees
TYPE: gland excretion from bees
MAGICKAL FORM: candles

It is believed that prayers said over burning candles made of pure beeswax are delivered straight to heaven or to the ears of God. Beeswax can also be used to fashion talismans, sacred seals, and pentagrams. Spread the beeswax out flat and carve the talisman or sigil into the wax. Throw it into a fire to activate the magick.

Beet

RULER: Saturn
TYPE: vegetable
MAGICKAL FORM: cooked beets, raw beet tops

Eat green beet tops on a Saturday to increase your income and create more job opportunities. Consuming beets is very good for your health and stamina and is said to prolong life span. Carve the names of two lovers into a whole beet and offer it to the goddess under a full moon to bring longevity to the relationship. According to the Kabbalah, eating beets on a new moon will eliminate your enemies.

Bell

RULER: element of spirit
TYPE: ritual tool
MAGICKAL FORM: the pitch, the shape

Always found on the witches' altar, the bell is a tool of summoning and dismissing. It is rung to call the coven to order. It is clanged to dismiss baneful spirits and chimed to call benevolent ones to the witch's aid. A bell's most important feature is its pitch and tone, which must be pleasing to the owner. The shape is also important and a matter of personal taste. Bells with owls on the stem are sacred to the goddess Hecate. Elephant-shaped bells ring out obstacles and are great clearing bells. Rooster bells wake up the dormant energies within the magician.

Belladonna, see Eye of Newt

Benzoin

RULER: Mercury
TYPE: plant resin
MAGICKAL FORM: resinous oil, powder

A gum resin from the Benjamin-bush or spicebush, benzoin is a fixative used to bind other magickal ingredients together when making incense or pastes. It is used in holy recipes and ceremonial magick and the powder can be sprinkled on any potion to make its power longer lasting.

Bergamot

RULER: Moon
TYPE: herb
MAGICKAL FORM: dried leaves, oil

The easiest way to obtain bergamot is in Earl Grey tea bags because the black tea is soaked or cured in pure oil of bergamot. The oil can also be purchased separately. This is one of the best protective agents of the atomic and nuclear age as it helps the user to avoid all disaster and provides warning before any surprise attack. Carry it when traveling or drink it whenever you feel in danger. Rub the oil into protection candles and light on a Monday night.

Beryl

RULER: Yahweh
TYPE: mineral
MAGICKAL FORM: polished and cut, assorted colors

One of the twelve gemstones on the breastplate of Aaron, the high priest of ancient Israel, this gemstone carries very high spiritual vibrations. Beryl is one of the stones used in kaballistic and ceremonial magick. Wear or carry it when you have lost your way and long for divine guidance. It also aids in important decision making and brings confidence with humility.

Betony, Wood

RULER: Mars
TYPE: herb
MAGICKAL FORM: live plant, dried bark

A very protective and healing plant, it is traditionally grown in a garden or around a home to ward off evil from inhabitants. Place under the pillow for protection from incubus or succubus or any night demons. Mix with lavender and burn to heal arguments between lovers.

Birch

RULER: Venus
TYPE: tree
MAGICKAL FORM: bark, birch beer

Add the cut bark to protection spells or drink birch beer if you feel you are under psychic attack. This is a great herb to use to banish fears and build courage. Birch also brings happiness.

Bittersweet

RULER: Saturn, Hecate, Pluto
TYPE: plant
MAGICKAL FORM: leaves and root

This infamous climbing weed puts a stranglehold on other plants in your garden. To choke out competition or to paralyze others from making a move against you, dig up the root, then dry and pulverize it. (Do not use a coffee grinder or food processor that you use for food preparations as this plant is poisonous!) Sprinkle this powder over the name or business card of a competitor and place in a ziplock bag in a dark and hidden place. To regain a position that has been lost, clip a climbing leaf and wrap it around a piece of paper upon which you have written the situation you wish to regain. Hang a whole root above a doorway to drive away evil.

Black

RULER: Hecate
TYPE: color
MAGICKAL FORM: clothing, candle, altar cloth

This is the color of the clergy, and witches use it to cloak themselves and to safeguard their mysteries. Black has a bad reputation and is often associated with evil workings, but the pure color can also be used for concentration, solitude, and deep meditation. It is also used to honor the Queen of the Witches or the dark crone aspect of the goddess.

Blackberry

RULER: Venus
TYPE: fruit
MAGICKAL FORM: whole berries, jam

Delicious and dark, this berry brings forth the lusty side of Venus and can heighten sexual pleasure and bring deeper bonding between couples. Blackberry is a favorite among S&M practitioners and fetishists. It brings the darker side of sexuality into play. Use it sparingly.

Bleeding Heart

RULER: Jesus, all sacrificed gods
TYPE: plant
MAGICKAL FORM: flower

Also known as Lady in the Bath, these tiny pink or white flowers resemble hearts with drops of blood at the bottom. They stir compassion and forgiveness and help to cure melancholy and depression. When grown in a garden, they are believed to lift sorrows from the household. Add several dozen to the bathwater to ease the pain of a broken heart.

Blood

RULER: Moon goddess
TYPE: human secretion
MAGICKAL FORM: menstrual, pricked from a finger

One of the most powerful ingredients in magickal spells, blood is used to bind, protect, and take oaths. In Wiccan initiation rites, blood is drawn from the finger and absorbed into a piece of red cord that has been used to take the measure of the initiate. It is kept by the priestess to ensure the initiate honors his or her oath of secrecy. In handfastings, or Wiccan marriages, blood is drawn from the wrists of the couple and the blood is mingled as the wrists are bound together, ensuring that the couple will be spiritually and magickally bonded. *Menstrual blood* is fed to a lover to force fidelity. It is also given as an offering to the goddess. In Gnostic masses, cakes of light are eaten with drops of menstrual or "wise" blood cooked into them. Add drops of your own blood to personal anointing oils to infuse them with power and protection. Do not share this oil with others.

Bloodroot

RULER: Mars
TYPE: herb
MAGICKAL FORM: root

Add to red ouanga bags along with other lust herbs to draw a male lover. Men can carry the root to increase virility. Place two roots in purple conjure bag to increase courage and promote fearlessness and increase physical energy. Do not take internally, as bloodroot is poisonous.

Bloodstone

RULER: Neptune, Jesus
TYPE: mineral
MAGICKAL FORM: polished

The martyr's gem is actually a stone of abundance and brings spiritual balance and good fortune to those who carry it. The oldest legends say the red flecks are the rays of the setting sun upon the ocean. It was later said that the stone was formed from drops of Christ's blood that fell upon a jasper at the foot of the cross. Bloodstone is used in invisibility spells. Rub heliotrope oil into the gem and then carry it within the pocket of your cloak. The wearer will then become, in some sense, "invisible."

Blue

RULER: Jupiter, Neptune, Mercury, Moon
TYPE: color
MAGICKAL FORM: candles, other magickal objects bearing this shade

Sensitivity, intellect, protection, calmness, benevolence, and wisdom are all invoked through the color blue. Eat blue foods, like blueberries or blue corn, to alleviate stress. Burn blue candles to get out of harm's way or bring a judgment in your favor. Visualize the color blue while taking a test, as it increases mental activity and relaxes and opens brain centers. Since it is traditional to surround your magickal circle with candles representing each of the four directions, and since blue is the color of water (west) and sky (east), use a blue candle to represent either of these quarters.

Blueberry

RULER: Moon
TYPE: fruit
MAGICKAL FORM: whole, crushed

Tinting the hands or feet with blueberry pulp is one of the strongest methods of protecting children. Never frighten youngsters with this ritual. Make a game of it. Throw some in a tub and let them have fun crushing them underfoot. Eat blueberries on a full moon to strengthen your aura and protect your physical body. New moon rituals with blueberries will strengthen your determination to commit to an exercise routine or carry through with any difficult project.

Bluestone

RULER: Moon
TYPE: copper mineral
MAGICKAL FORM: laundry blueing balls

Most familiar in 1950s laundry rooms, blueing balls were added to the wash to whiten clothes. In southern, voodoo, and hoodoo magick, they are added to the bathwater to cleanse the spirit of evil. Dissolve three blueing balls in a tub of hot water and soak for ten minutes to remove unwanted negative thoughts or evil energy aimed at you. Carry blueing balls in a mojo bag for luck in gambling.

Bok Choy

RULER: Jupiter, Buddha
TYPE: vegetable
MAGICKAL FORM: sautéed

Eat bok choy to clear away bad karma and obstacles in your path to prosperity. This is a great vegetable to incorporate into rituals to bless a new business endeavor and clear the path before you set out on it. Bok choy is also a great magickal ingredient to uncross bad fortune in life. It often brings insight as to why prosperity is not flowing your way and will help you make positive changes to clear blocks from your path.

Borage

RULER: Jupiter
TYPE: herb
MAGICKAL FORM: blossoms, dried leaves

Place the fresh blossoms on an altar to bring luck and power to your spells. Sprinkle crushed dried leaves around the workplace for inspiration and business expansion. Drink the tea to increase psychic abilities.

Bread

RULER: Moon goddesses or gods of grain
TYPE: food
MAGICKAL FORM: whole round, phallic shaped

On the autumn equinox, cut phallic-shaped bread into pieces and then bury them in the earth. This rite symbolizes the sacrificed grain god whose seed will return to the earth to fertilize it and bring new life in the spring. On the full moon, place round bread on the altar and bless it for prosperity and fertility. Offer half the bread to the earth and share the other half with coven members. In many cultures, prayers are often said over bread, which is considered sacred, before eating it. It represents the union of humankind and the divine. In some cases it is representative solely of the divine, but by ingesting it, humans are able to take in the divinity. Bake and eat dark breads full of grains for prosperity.

Bristles

RULER: time
TYPE: hair
MAGICKAL FORM: cut, shaven, plucked

Use the coarse hairs taken from a man's beard growth to increase virility. Mix the hairs with talcum powder and aloe and rub into your body on a Tuesday. Bristles on the chin of a witch are said to denote wisdom. When plucked, the wisdom increases. When left intact, the eye turns inward and dementia occurs.

Broccoli

RULER: Moon
TYPE: vegetable
MAGICKAL FORM: whole head

Broccoli is a preventative for disease. Eat to safeguard your health. You can also eat it whenever you feel endangered, as its protective vibe quickly enters your aura. Because it is a green vegetable, broccoli is also a prosperity food. Steam, salt, and eat it on full moons to increase and protect your income.

Broom

RULER: God, Goddess
TYPE: household item
MAGICKAL FORM: corn broom is best

The witches' broom is used for flying. There are two versions of the origin of this belief. The first claims that flying on the broom is a myth that arose from witnessing pagans jumping up and down in a field to encourage crops to grow. Someone mistakenly thought they were trying to fly. The second version claims that a broom handle was rubbed with hallucinogenic ointments and inserted into the vagina so that the substance would quickly enter the bloodstream and bring about flight or out-of-body experiences. Riding the broom was also an old euphemism for a woman being on top during sexual intercourse. This represented female or witch power. In any case, the witches' broom is used to bless the union of a couple with fertility. At the end of the handfasting rite, the couple jumps the broom to bless their union. The broom handle represents the male and the skirt of the broom represents the female. Witches always keep a broom skirt-side up in their homes to honor the goddess. The witches' broom is also used for sweeping out negativity from a space. Begin at the front door and sweep counterclockwise in a circle around the room. When you reach the point of origin, open the door and sweep out all the negativity. Note: the room should be physically clean before the ritual sweeping.

Broom Tops

RULER: Hecate
TYPE: herb
MAGICKAL FORM: dried

Stuff a generous helping of this herb into a cloth bag and place it under your pillow to get rid of nightmares. Add it to flying recipes to gain the sight for psychic visions. Broom tops or Scotch broom is also used in weather magick.

Brown

RULER: Saturn
TYPE: color
MAGICKAL FORM: candle, cloth

This color is used in magick to gain strength and to become more connected to the earth. Brown autumn leaves placed upon an altar will enable greater endurance and protection during the winter months. Burning brown candles normally separates individuals, but in Pennsylvania hex magick, the color is used to promote serious relationships between men and women. It is the color of deep abiding and committed love.

Brussels Sprouts

RULER: Moon
TYPE: vegetable
MAGICKAL FORM: steamed

On a full moon, steam and eat brussels sprouts to make your money last longer. Eat them salted for protection and peace between family members.

Buckeye

RULER: Jupiter
TYPE: plant
MAGICKAL FORM: dried seedpod

Carry for luck. Rub with bay oil and wrap a dollar bill around the buckeye. Make sure the pyramid side of the dollar is facing out. Place the buckeye with the dollar wrapped around it in your wallet or purse to draw money and luck. For gamblers, rub the buckeye with cinnamon oil and carry in the pocket to increase your luck at winning bets.

Buckwheat

RULER: Venus
TYPE: grain
MAGICKAL FORM: seeds, flour

When searching for employment, make pancakes using buckwheat flour on a new moon. Eat while picturing getting the job you want. On a full moon, sprinkle the seeds over your wallet to increase wealth or to get a raise. Add buckwheat seeds to other grains and eat on Fridays to draw money or financial opportunities into your life.

Burdock

RULER: Venus
TYPE: plant
MAGICKAL FORM: root, leaves

An herb of health and power, the burdock is also very protective. Eat the root or use it to brew a tea. Or carry it in your pocket. Add it to a bucket of water and sprinkle around the home or do a floor wash to cleanse a space of negativity. A burdock wash is great while recovering from illness. It helps ward off contagions on both the physical and the spiritual planes.

Butter

RULER: Venus, Hathor, and Lakshmi
TYPE: dairy
MAGICKAL FORM: raw, cooked

Nurturing and protective, butter is also eaten to attract wealth. Melt on dark green vegetables and eat for prosperity. Cook with eggs for protection. Butter on bread brings material and spiritual sustenance. The most powerful form of butter is *ghee* or clarified butter. It represents the goddess in her most nurturing and protective form. Rub ghee into the body for peace, protection, enlightenment, and goddess energy. It is also sacred to Lakshmi, the Hindu goddess of wealth, and will bestow her blessings upon you. Eat ghee on full moons for prosperity and sustenance.

Butterfly

RULER: Mercury
TYPE: insect
MAGICKAL FORM: live

Never kill a butterfly or your creative energy will die. Express your wishes while observing them in gardens. As they flutter from flower to flower, speak out your desires for love. If a butterfly touches your skin, someone you like will flirt with you within the week and your social standing will greatly improve within the month. Touching the wings of a butterfly is said to make you, in some sense, "immortal."

C

Cabbage

RULER: Moon
TYPE: vegetable
MAGICKAL FORM: whole head

Round vegetables invoke the power of the full moon and should be blessed whole before they are cut and cooked. Hold the cabbage in both hands and speak out a prayer in your own words concerning fullness, success, or the completion you desire in a specific area of your life. Use *white cabbage* for spiritual wholeness, *green cabbage* for prosperity, *purple cabbage* for power, and *red cabbage* for love matters. After blessing the cabbage, carve your name into its side. Then cook whole or dice for raw dishes.

Cactus

RULER: Mars
TYPE: plant
MAGICKAL FORM: leaves, juice

The spiked leaves of the cactus are believed to prick any evil entities that enter the home. It is also regarded as a survival plant and its energy supports those going through a rough time. Keep the plant in your home to protect and strengthen the will. Use cactus juice in love potions to increase sexual stamina.

Calamus

RULER: Moon
TYPE: herb
MAGICKAL FORM: root, powder, oil

Rub calamus oil into your feet to attract spirit or animal guides to accompany you on vision quests. Burn or carry the powder or root to travel safely in the physical and spiritual realms. Chew on a bit of the sweet root to bring clear vision and strengthen the psychic senses. Offer to the goddess to protect you on your path.

Calcite

RULER: Mercury
TYPE: mineral
MAGICKAL FORM: various colors

This slated or tiled gemstone is a very powerful tool for opening the brain's psychic centers. Hold this stone to deepen thoughts and increase the psychic senses. It is especially useful for astral travel. *Gold calcite* improves memory. *Green calcite* promotes physical and emotional health and balance. *White calcite* brings eloquence; hold it while composing a prayer. *Gray calcite* neutralizes negativity. Use *red calcite* to get in touch with your feelings and open your heart.

Camelia

RULER: Venus
TYPE: flower
MAGICKAL FORM: flower, oil

Working with this scent or flower brings forth inner beauty. Adding the oil or flower to the bath causes the skin and aura to glow. Add camelia to love potions when self-esteem and self-confidence are needed. It's a great scent to bring the wallflower out of his or her shell.

Camphor

RULER: Moon, Buddha
TYPE: extract from tree
MAGICKAL FORM: oil, whole chunks

Obtained from the evergreen tree, this fragrant white compound holds many spiritual properties. In voodoo rituals, it is burned for love and attraction. It is one of the most sacred substances to offer to the moon goddess on a new moon to thank her for her abundant blessings. Camphor is also used in cleansing and purification rituals. Use it to get rid of unwanted passions or unwanted admirers. It is one of the seven substances most sacred to Buddha and meditation upon it, or in its presence, will bring enlightenment.

Candles

RULER: fire
TYPE: wax, paraffin
MAGICKAL FORM: various shapes and colors

One of the most used tools of spellcraft and magick, candles are essentially vessels that carry and deliver prayers. Candles are also used on the altar to honor gods and goddesses and the four quarters or elements (earth, air, fire, and water). Candle colors and shapes have different meanings. *Red* candles are for love or energy, and *pink* ones are burned for flirtation, harmony, or emotional healing. Burning an *orange* candle brings success and motivation; a *brown* candle, power and stability. *Black* candles are burned for protection or cursing. *White* candles are used to clear the path, for protection and healing. *Blue* candles bring peace and protection, *green* candles prosperity. *Purple* candles provide power and wisdom, *yellow* candles success, fame, and glory. *Male* and *female figure* candles are burned for love, protection, separation, or healing. *Cat* candles are burned for love and luck. *Cross* candles are burned for protection and used as devotionals. *Seven-knot* candles are burned while making wishes as each knot burns. *Seven-color* candles are devotionals for the seven orishas, or Yoruban gods and goddesses. *Skull* candles are used for hexing or healing depending on the color. *Witch* candles are burned for love spells. *Reversible* or *double-action* candles are black and red and burned to return evil to the sender.

Candy

RULER: Ellegua, Ganesh, Squat
TYPE: food
MAGICKAL FORM: red-and-white-striped peppermints, caramels, coconut candies, milk candies, chocolate

Specific sweets make quite an impression on certain deities. Ellegua or Legba, the Yoruban god of the crossroads, loves striped peppermints, caramels, and coconut- or rum-flavored candies. Leave them in multiples of three in a crossroads and ask him to clear your path of obstacles. The Hindu god Ganesh, remover of obstacles, is fond of old-fashioned milk candies and will remove your blocks in exchange for them. The modern urban goddess Squat rules parking spots. She'll get you a legal one if you chant "Squat, Squat please give me a spot," but she expects to be rewarded with a piece of chocolate left at the curbside front wheel. Without this sweet offering she may send a tow truck after your car.

Cantaloupe

RULER: Yemanja, Venus
TYPE: fruit
MAGICKAL FORM: whole

This is the slippery fruit of adultery. Split open the shell and carve your name and the name of a married man or woman you are after into the juicy pulp of the fruit. Eat half and offer half to the ocean by bringing it to the shoreline. Wait and see how the tides turn. If the sea swallows the melon and takes it far out, the one you desire will leave the marriage to be with you. If the sea spits back the melon to the shore, he or she will always return to the marriage but continue to see you on the side. The petitioner may continue to bathe in the juice of a melon to further influence the desired one to surrender to his or her seductions. The cantaloupe is also offered whole to Yemanja, the goddess of the sea, along with any request for fulfillment in love.

Capers

RULER: Hermes
TYPE: flower bud
MAGICKAL FORM: pickled

Wit and charm are the properties of the clever caper. Eat them to improve your social skills and popularity. The caper is also known to be a favorite of liars, cheaters, and thieves. By creating an aura of believability, seduction, and sleuth, the caper helps them to pull the wool over unsuspecting eyes.

Caraway

RULER: Mercury
TYPE: herb
MAGICKAL FORM: seed

Also known as rye seed, caraway is an herb of communication and information. Eating these seeds while doing research will quickly lead you to the facts you need. Ball up the seeds in tinfoil and touch a phone or computer with it to compel someone to call or e-mail you.

Cardamom

RULER: Venus, Mars, Lakshmi
TYPE: spice
MAGICKAL FORM: pods

Hold some under your tongue before kissing someone. Cardamom is an aphrodisiac and draws love and sensuality into your life. Use the *white* pods for matters of the heart; crush and add to any love spell to invigorate the results. The *green* pods bring the blessing of wealth and luck when sucked on or added to incense blends for prosperity. Burn the powdered seed on a full moon for a financial boon.

Cards

RULER: gods and goddesses of divination
TYPE: fortune-telling tool
MAGICKAL FORM: Tarot or playing cards

Witches and gypsies employ cards with symbols to read the past, present, and future outcomes of events. Each card has a specific meaning that is memorized, but experienced readers use them as tools to trigger their own unique psychic impressions. All cards should be blessed by passing them through the four elements before being used as divining tools. Sprinkle salt (earth) over them, sprinkle a small amount of water,

pass them through incense smoke (air), and pass them over a burning candle (fire) to rid them of any negative or harmful energies.

Carnation

RULER: Capricorn, Saturn
TYPE: flower
MAGICKAL FORM: fresh, dried, oil

Used to remove hexes and negative energy, the carnation is especially good for clearing out love problems. Brush flowers down your body to cleanse. After reaching the feet, break the stems to trap and hold the negative energy. Add white and red carnations or essential oil to bathwater to stabilize your love life. This flower also helps relieve the depression of winter. Keep red carnations on the altar to increase your energy level and to create more optimism in life.

Carnelian

RULER: Ra, Osiris, Horus
TYPE: mineral
MAGICKAL FORM: loose stone, set in silver

This stone is associated with karma and the law of return. It brings reckoning and acceptance. When carried or worn, it opens the heart and promotes kindness and consideration of others. It is the best stone to meditate upon to remember past lives.

Carob

RULER: Venus
TYPE: plant
MAGICKAL FORM: bean, powder, chocolate substitute

Eat carob, a food of friendship, to attract loving, trusting friends into your life. Carob is also very protective; have some on Fridays to steer you clear of harm's way. It is a great ingredient for children. Healthier than chocolate, it will manifest magick to keep them safe and attract nonsexual love.

Carrot

RULER: Mars
TYPE: vegetable
MAGICKAL FORM: whole, leaves, juice, oil, seed

In whichever form you consume it, carrot improves not only the eyesight but also your psychic vision. It lends energy, improves drive and motivation, and increases willpower and sexual stamina. The seeds are the most lust-producing part of the carrot. Eat on Tuesdays to gain the most benefit.

Cascaria

RULER: voodoo and Santeria deities
TYPE: egg product
MAGICKAL FORM: powdered

Made from powdered eggshells, this magickal white chalk is one of the oldest tools of ritual. It is used to draw veves or seals on hard ground or wooden floors. In Africa, elaborate figures are sketched to draw down the power of their deities. Cascaria is also added to protection and purification blends and is sometimes offered to deities for forgiveness or as guilt offerings. Easily found in botanicas or occult shops, cascaria is the most powerful kind of chalk you can use to draw a pentagram or magick circle.

Cassava

RULER: Mayan gods
TYPE: plant
MAGICKAL FORM: root, leaves, tapioca

This staple food is eaten to ward off poverty and prevent harm from enemies. Cassava chips can be found in health food stores. Tapioca pudding is made from this plant; eat some to conquer enemies and fears.

Catnip

RULER: Venus, Baust
TYPE: plant
MAGICKAL FORM: dried

Aside from being the cat's favorite drug, catnip is an aphrodisiac. When added to love spells, it energizes them and speeds up the results. Sprinkle catnip under the bed for a lusty night.

Cats

RULER: Baust
TYPE: animal
MAGICKAL FORM: alive, whiskers, hair

This animal is the most common of the witches' familiars. They are very sensitive to occult workings and wise in the ways of the goddess. In order to make the cat a familiar, it must taste the blood of the witch. The correct way to do this is to let the cat become your familiar in his or her own time. You will know when this occurs, as he or she will take a good hard bite out of your hand, cheek, or leg and draw blood. Voilà! You are now bonded for eternal life. When a cat drops a whisker, place it on the altar for good luck. It is very bad luck to cut or pluck a whisker from a cat. Cat hair may be obtained by rubbing the back against the grain. Add the hairs to gamblers' luck potions to increase your chances of winning. *Black cats* are very lucky indeed and you will be blessed when one crosses your path. *Red cats* and *calicos* bring money. A *gray cat* will protect you and a *Siamese cat* will bring laughter into your life.

Cauldron

RULER: Cerridwen
TYPE: altar tool
MAGICKAL FORM: iron pot

A sacred symbol of the feminine, the cauldron represents the womb of the goddess. The witch mixes all her magick in this pot from which the goddess Cerridwen drew all her wisdom and wisecraft. In medieval times, cauldrons were used for cooking and placed inside the hearth fire. In modern Wicca, the cauldron is made of cast iron and placed on the altar as the representation of air. Incense is burned within it. On the Beltane witches' sabbat (May 1), coven members leap over a fiery cauldron set outdoors to receive the blessings of the season.

Cauliflower

RULER: Moon
TYPE: vegetable
MAGICKAL FORM: whole

Use this vegetable for protection in times of danger. The cauliflower should be blessed whole before preparing. Hold it in your hands up to a full moon and say a prayer for protection in your own words. Salt before cooking. Serve to children to keep them safe from harm. Eat in preparation before encountering a perilous situation. The cauliflower also calms down tempers and is a great dish to serve to overcome agitation in the household.

Caviar

RULER: Neptune, Venus
TYPE: fish eggs
MAGICKAL FORM: black, gray, red

An expensive and extravagant aphrodisiac, caviar works quickly to create a sexy mood. Eat the *red eggs* for lust. The *gray eggs* bring surprises and the *black eggs* deepen emotional and sexual bonds.

Cedar

RULER: Sun, Venus
TYPE: tree
MAGICKAL FORM: bark chips, oil

One of the holiest of woods, cedar is considered feminine and receptive in nature. Cedar denotes great beauty, majesty, and strength. It is highly protective when worn and draws money, good health, and well-being when burned. Add to love potions when strength is needed to overcome hardships. Cedar opens up the intuitive channels and brings forth compassion and humility. It is a true symbol of prosperity.

Celery

RULER: Mars, Mercury
TYPE: vegetable
MAGICKAL FORM: stalks, seed, oil

Eat *raw* celery to remove blocks and fears and to promote weight loss. Cook the stalks in soup for love. Use *celery seed* to increase male virility. Men can either eat it or add it to poppets in sympathetic magic spells. Rub the *oil* into fingers or the third eye to increase communication skills.

Chalk

RULER: associated with voodoo deities
TYPE: mineral
MAGICKAL FORM: white powder, stick

Draw a circle on the floor with chalk when you wish to create a safe space or sacred environment. Chalk is often used in voodoo rituals to draw veves or seals. The original graffiti was written in chalk. It is a great substance to work with when you need to be secret in your rites. Witches often drew chalk circles or pentagrams and then erased them when the ritual was completed. To cause a seal or circle to "become invisible" after it has been worked is considered very powerful. Using chalk allows our magic to escape into the ethers and do its work.

Chamomile

RULER: Sun
TYPE: plant
MAGICKAL FORM: cut flowers

One of the strongest healing herbs, chamomile also relieves stress and brings happiness. Brew in a tea and drink to lift your spirits or calm your nerves. Bathe in the flowers to soothe tensions and solve problems of the heart.

Chants

RULER: various
TYPE: words
MAGICKAL FORM: rhyming

The words of the witch are most powerful and magick in and of themselves. Chants that rhyme hold extra potency. The chant is a form of prayer and witches use them to raise energy. Many witches run or dance while chanting, as this doubles the energy produced. As the chant reaches its climax, raise your arms high into the air with energy reaching through your fingertips. This releases the energy into the heavens. Then place your hands upon the earth to ground the energy and make sure it returns to the realm of the physical.

Cheese

RULER: Saturn, Moon, Venus
TYPE: dairy food
MAGICKAL FORM: aged, soft

Aged cheeses are ruled by Saturn and eaten for power and persistence. *Stinky* cheeses increase your influence upon others. These cheeses are best eaten on Saturdays. *Soft* cheeses are ruled by the Moon or Venus and are added to love recipes or eaten alone for nurturing. They should be eaten on Mondays or Fridays. *Moldy* cheese should not be eaten, but can be used as a talisman to solve money problems. Bury in the ground on a new moon and wish that your financial obstacles be removed.

Cherry

RULER: Sun
TYPE: fruit
MAGICKAL FORM: flesh, pit, stem, jam

Eat this fruit on Sundays to chase away the blues. The cherry brings gladness and cures depression. It also boosts self-confidence and is good for lifting morale. It is customary to pull the stems and make a wish and then spit out the seeds to see how far your wish will go. When the fruit is not in season, eat cherry jam for happiness.

Chervil

RULER: Ceres
TYPE: herb
MAGICKAL FORM: tonic, fresh leaves

Eat for renewal and to rejuvenate the mind, body, and spirit. Place fresh sprigs on a spring altar for inspiration and creativity.

Chestnut

RULER: Venus
TYPE: nut
MAGICKAL FORM: roasted

As prescribed in the popular song, roast this nut over an open fire. Carve your initials and those of your loved one into the chestnut before roasting. As the shell splits, the hearts will open and make room for love. The chestnut promotes trust and open communication and is also offered to the gods in gratitude for their help.

Chickweed

RULER: Mercury
TYPE: plant
MAGICKAL FORM: leaves, flowers

Carry dried chickweed in the pockets to open up travel opportunities to faraway lands. Add to salads and eat or bathe in to be able to communicate with birds.

Chicory

RULER: Sun
TYPE: herb
MAGICKAL FORM: bark, leaves

This happy herb summons feelings of happiness and contentment and helps to banish turmoil and depression. Carry or sprinkle, or drink tea when you are confused about your path. Chicory helps you make positive beneficial decisions in life and drives away unhappiness and insecurity.

Chives

RULER: Mars
TYPE: herb
MAGICKAL FORM: fresh

Invoke mischief with the chive. It is a great herb to use when action is needed. It stimulates and prods, and although its effects may be uncomfortable, the end results are always positive. Chop and add to salads when you want to stir things up.

Chocolate

RULER: Venus
TYPE: spice
MAGICKAL FORM: dark

Sacred to many Aztec and Mayan deities, chocolate is a power drug. It holds the property of love. It has been scientifically proven that it raises the endorphin level in the body. Dark chocolate is the best form to use in magic for romantic or sexual love. Milk chocolate is best for nurturing and friend-ship.

Chrysanthemum

RULER: goddess of seasons and change, fire
TYPE: plant
MAGICKAL FORM: flower

This multicolored fall bloom holds cooling properties. The Chinese brew tea from its flowers to reduce fevers. For magickal purposes sprinkle the petals around a space to stop arguments and calm fiery tempers. Add whole fresh flowers with stems to the bathwater to get rid of a bad mood. Before exiting the bath, break all the stems of the flowers to cut off the negative energy they have absorbed. Mums are the flower of choice to decorate the altar for autumn equinox rituals.

Cilantro

RULER: Mercury
TYPE: herb
MAGICKAL FORM: fresh, dried

The distinctive taste and smell of cilantro "wakes up" food and the taste buds. Ingesting it brings greater awareness and strengthens wit and mental capacity. Eat on Wednesdays to increase your creativity and communication skills. Sprinkle dried cilantro around green candles, then light to attract money for creative or artistic enterprises. Carry fresh sprigs in the pocket on job interviews for success.

Cinnamon

RULER: Sun, Mercury, all gods and goddesses of victory
TYPE: spice
MAGICKAL FORM: powder, sticks, oil

A favorite of many gods and goddesses, cinnamon powder is sprinkled on offerings to attract attention and win the favor of the gods. Add the oil or powder to any money or success blend to bring swift results. Before getting out of bed in the morning, rub a dab of the pure essential oil into the soles of your feet and you will be led to money during the course of your day. Chew cinnamon sticks to summon winged Mercury for luck in creative endeavors. For victory and to increase your chances of winning, dust your hands with cinnamon powder or add a few drops of cinnamon oil to the bathwater on a Sunday or any day at sunrise.

Circle

RULER: four watchtowers, gods and goddesses
TYPE: invocation
MAGICKAL FORM: sacred space invoked

The witches' church or temple might be outdoors, in a small apartment or a grand one, or in the stuffy backroom of an occult shop—it can be anyplace where she has drawn the circle and created the sacred space. Although some witches physically draw a chalk circle on the ground, the witches' circle is most commonly drawn or invoked in the air using a sword or dagger or possibly just the index and middle finger of the right hand. She circles clockwise three times speaking the sacred words of invocation with her right arm outstretched and tracing the round through the air. Once this space is created, the gods enter and allow the ritual to be worked with optimum success and power. No evil can enter within. Once the magick rite or worship has been completed, the circle is opened and she returns to the mundane.

Citrine

RULER: Mercury
TYPE: mineral
MAGICKAL FORM: cut, unpolished

This is the stone of harmony and success. It removes creative blocks and prevents emotional and physical stagnation. Carry one when you need to be stimulated or to create more self-confidence. This stone holds the vibration of generosity and will help you to take greater pleasure in everyday life.

Citron

RULER: Yahweh, Kwan-yin
TYPE: fruit
MAGICKAL FORM: whole

Prized in the ancient world by many cultures, the lemony citron has both a fragrant smell and a good taste. It represents a person whose knowledge or study permeates and influences his or her actions. The citron is the fruit of choice for raising consciousness and propelling an individual into reaching his or her full potential. It sweetens the lessons of life and makes them easily incorporated. In the Chinese tradition, the fruit is placed in a bowl on an altar in the most predominant room of the house. As its fragrance spreads, it will influence those in the dwelling to be the best they can be. In kabbalistic or ceremonial magick, the fruit is energized by holding in both hands and vibrating the name of the Hebrew god—"Yahweh," "Adonai," or "Y'hovah."

Citronella

RULER: Moon
TYPE: plant
MAGICKAL FORM: oil

This oil makes a great bug repellant. In magick it is used to drive away evil or anything "bugging you." Rub into white candles and burn for protection and shielding. Wear a dab of the oil on the wrists, back of the neck, behind the knees, and on the bottoms of the feet to keep you protected on your spiritual and physical path.

Civet

RULER: Pan
TYPE: animal secretion
MAGICKAL FORM: real or synthetic oil or balm

Although illegal in many countries, it is still possible to obtain real civet. It is a favorite ingredient of perfumers and is derived from the spray of the male civet cat. Synthetic blends are easily obtainable and appropriate for magickal blends. (In 2004, the Chinese government banned the use of products derived from civet cat as they were connected with the spreading of SARS [severe acute respiratory syndrome]. Because of these findings, I would recommend using only the synthetic substitutes.) The oil is worn to increase sexual magnetism, activity, and opportunity. This is one of the best oils of love for gay men.

Clementine

RULER: Venus, Sun, Bast
TYPE: fruit
MAGICKAL FORM: fruit, peel

Eat this fruit on Sundays to strengthen the immune system and promote good health. Or consume some on Fridays to attract more friends into your life. Serve clementines at parties to invoke spontaneity and fun. Feed them to children (or adults) who need help in overcoming shyness. Carry the dried peel in your pocket to increase self-confidence.

Clove

RULER: Jupiter
TYPE: spice
MAGICKAL FORM: whole or powdered herb, oil

Use in commanding, compelling, and controlling formulas to get another to do your bidding. Chew on whole cloves while trying to collect money owed to you. Visualize the debt being paid and when you have a clear picture of this, spit out the clove. Add the powder to success formulas for an extra kick. Rub the oil on the thigh for sexual prowess.

Clover

RULER: Jupiter
TYPE: plant
MAGICKAL FORM: three-, four-, five-leaf

A symbol of luck, leprechauns, and wishes, the shamrock or cloverleaf is a powerful talisman to carry. The three-leaf clover represents the Holy Trinity—Father, Son, and Holy Spirit, or Maiden, Mother, and Crone. The four-leaf clover represents hope, faith, love, and luck. The five-leaf clover represents the pentagram or five-pointed star and multiplies the blessings of the shamrock by five.

Coconut

RULER: Moon, Ellegua
TYPE: fruit
MAGICKAL FORM: whole, split, shell, flesh, milk

To break a love spell, kick a coconut hard until it splits. You will then have broken the magick spell cast upon you. Coconut bowls are sacred to the Moon and make wonderful libation bowls for offerings to the goddess. Eat the meat of the coconut for purification. Add the milk to bathwater for cleansing and nurturing. Leave offerings of coconut to Ellegua at the crossroads or behind the door of a dwelling and ask him to remove your obstacles.

Coffee

RULER: Mars, Saturn
TYPE: plant
MAGICKAL FORM: whole or ground beans, brewed

Sprinkling ground coffee in the four corners of a room, or brewing coffee in the room, will make the occupants work harder. Add a brewed pot of coffee to the bathwater for energy. It will give you extra stamina and push you to forge ahead and work longer hours. The coffee bath is more beneficial than drinking it because it will not cause undue stress and there is no risk of overdosing. Carry whole coffee beans in the pocket for success in love.

Cohosh, Black

RULER: Venus and Saturn
TYPE: plant
MAGICKAL FORM: root, leaves

This is an abortive herb used to regulate the menstrual cycle. Do not use if pregnant. Cohosh is a protective and healing herb added to protection ouangas to drive away evil. Also called black snakeroot, rub the root with tonka or vanilla oil and carry in the pocket to increase sales or uncover financial opportunities.

Coins

RULER: Sun, Moon, Venus
TYPE: metal
MAGICKAL FORM: symbols on coins

The Sun rules gold or gold-colored coins. The Moon rules silver or silver-colored coins. Venus rules copper or copper-colored coins. Coins placed in a bowl of water on an altar with green candles burning will bring more money into your life. The water should be changed every three days. Coins can be carried in the pocket or purse as lucky talismans. Solar disks, lunar crescents, pigs, ships, pyramids, and elephants are all symbols that draw incredible prosperity. It is also important that the symbol on the coin be pleasing or uniquely symbolic to you. Old and smoothly worn coins are very powerful talismans for success.

Collard Greens

RULER: Mars
TYPE: vegetable
MAGICKAL FORM: steamed

Eat this vegetable on Tuesdays to find work during the week. This is a fast-luck formula and draws moneymaking opportunities quickly, though you must be willing to work for it.

Coltsfoot

RULER: Venus, Native American deities
TYPE: plant
MAGICKAL FORM: dried

Used for soothing sore throats, coltsfoot is also smoked to bring up phlegm from the lungs, or to quit cigarette smoking. The smoke is also sacred to Native American deities and brings blessings when blown to the six directions—north, east, south, west, above, and below. Coltsfoot is added to love spells to attract a soul mate.

Comfrey

RULER: Sun
TYPE: plant
MAGICKAL FORM: root

Carry the root to create a calming effect or sprinkle some shavings into your shoes so you will walk safely on your path. Comfrey makes a great travel talisman and can also be used in healing spells.

Copal

RULER: solar deities
TYPE: tree resin
MAGICKAL FORM: beads, tears

Burn this incense for purification and to contact the spirits of the dead. Mexican churches burn copal on the Day of the Dead to help the souls of the deceased reconnect with their loved ones on the earth plane. It makes a great meditation incense and increases psychic sight.

Copper

RULER: Venus
TYPE: mineral
MAGICKAL FORM: bracelets, chunks, rounded balls

This soft metal heals joints and conducts energy through the body. Copper opens channels for love and, when used in magick spells, attracts a soul mate. Wear or carry the ore to find happiness and fulfillment in your heart. It is one of the best minerals to place on an altar of Venus to draw her energy into your magick.

Coral

RULER: Venus, Neptune
TYPE: mineral
MAGICKAL FORM: white, pink, red

As a product of the sea, coral is connected with the element of water and the emotions or unconscious. *White coral* opens the door to the subconscious and brings vivid dreams when placed under the pillow. Wear *pink coral* for emotional healing. *Red coral* flames the passions; give it to someone you have a crush on to get him or her to like you back.

Cords

RULER: the goddess
TYPE: ritual tool
MAGICKAL FORM: white, red, black

In Wicca cords are used for binding and raising energy. Within the circle the initiate is taught the lessons of the craft while bound with three cords. Restricting the blood flow, which must be done under supervision, opens and raises the initiate's psychic centers. Cords are also knotted in spells to bind the magick. Perform binding spells for power and control, as well as to keep evil influences locked up. For a simple cord spell, tie seven knots in a red cord and repeat your wish seven times. The cord should then be burned to release the energy and the magick. Then gather the ash from the cord and rub it between your hands while calling out your wish seven more times. Finally, press your hands into the earth to invoke manifestation of the wish.

Coriander

RULER: Mercury, Mars
TYPE: spice
MAGICKAL FORM: seeds

Pop the seeds into your mouth on a Wednesday to increase your intelligence and mental alertness. Crack the seeds with your teeth and listen to the sound they make as this stimulates brain activity. Coriander is also used in lust and love spells. On a Tuesday, sprinkle the powdered seed over a male or female figure candle representing a person you desire. Light the candle and let it burn to completion. Continue this ritual every Tuesday until you have attracted this person into your life.

Cork

RULER: Bacchus
TYPE: tree bark
MAGICKAL FORM: bottle stopper

Cork is an essential ingredient for genie owners. Magic potions or oils sealed in a cork bottle are said to hold their powers longer. Use cork to make a love talisman when you feel your relationship is being threatened. Save a cork from a bottle of wine. Make sure it is stained with a bit of purple. Carve your name and your partner's name deep into the cork. Light a red candle and drip the wax over the cork until it is covered completely. Stuff the cork into a red cloth bag and hide it under the bed. Your relationship will be protected.

Corn

RULER: Sun, Aztec and Mayan deities, Earth Mother
TYPE: vegetable
MAGICKAL FORM: on or off the cob, popped, white, yellow, blue, red

Many cultures gave corn, which is regarded as a food of prosperity, protection, and spirituality, a special god or goddess of its own. Eat *yellow corn* on the summer solstice (June 21) for blessings of prosperity. Consume *white corn* for spiritual insight. Scatter *blue corn meal* to purify and bless a space. Hang *red corn* above doorways at harvest time (September to October) to protect rewards that have been reaped. *Corn on the cob* represents the phallic gods and draws creative or sexual energy. Financial or love wishes that are shouted out as *popcorn* is popping will come true. *Cornsilk* is a very powerful ingredient when added to love spells; it is designed to attract the person you desire.

Cornucopia

RULER: Zeus
TYPE: horn-shaped vessel
MAGICKAL FORM: overflowing

According to legend, the original cornucopia was the horn of the goat Amalthea. From it flowed a never-ending source of milk that fed and nurtured the infant Zeus. It is a tradition to fill horn-shaped baskets with fruits, nuts, and gourds for the harvest or fall altar. The horn should never be empty but should always have bounty pouring from it. Fill a cornucopia with coins and keep it on a money altar to ensure that your source of income continues to flow. It is one of the strongest talismans of prosperity.

Cotton

RULER: Moon
TYPE: plant
MAGICKAL FORM: woven, cotton balls

In southern lore, if you shape a piece of cotton into the initial of the one you love and lost and hold it in your lap, this person will return to you. Cotton brings good luck and it is the best material to use to create an ouanga bag to hold roots and talismans for magick spells. Burn a piece of cotton or soak it in camphor oil when you need rain.

Cowslip

RULER: Venus
TYPE: herb
MAGICKAL FORM: fresh or dried flowers

Carry to reunite with a lost love. Brings friendship and cures depression. Always expect a pleasant surprise to cheer you up when working with cowslip.

Crab

RULER: Venus
TYPE: shellfish
MAGICKAL FORM: meat, shell

Eat crabmeat to protect home and family. Use the shell of the *horseshoe crab* for real estate magick. Stuff the empty shell with lavender and sage to protect your dwelling. This is particularly effective when you are in danger of losing a space because of financial problems. If you are buying or renting property and need to come up with a down payment, stuff the crab shell with cinnamon sticks, bay leaves, and sea salt.

Cranberry

RULER: Saturn
TYPE: fruit
MAGICKAL FORM: whole, juice

Depending on how they are used, cranberries will either bond people together during tough times or create hardships that tear people apart. Drink the juice with your partner on the dark moon to keep the relationship free of trouble and going strong. Place a circle of cranberries around a brown or black candle and call out the names of two individuals who need to be separated while the candle burns. Continue the ritual until you obtain results.

Crocus

RULER: Venus
TYPE: plant
MAGICKAL FORM: flower, bulb

Blow into the face of the flower and make a love wish. Plant the bulbs to protect a love relationship from infidelity.

Croissant (or Media Luna)

RULER: Moon
TYPE: bread
MAGICKAL FORM: crescent shaped

There is much controversy over the true origin of the croissant, but the fact is that these "moon cakes" were offered to the lunar goddess of Mesopotamia long before the French pastry chefs claimed to have invented it. Eat the crescent moon cakes for protection on the dark moon, energy on the new moon, and blessings on the full moon. Offer them as thanks to the moon goddess whenever she fulfills a request.

Crossroad

RULER: Hecate, Ellegua
TYPE: physical place
MAGICKAL FORM: sacred space

Times Square in New York City is known as the "Crossroads of the World." A true urban crossroads is any intersection where four roads meet and then continue outward unobstructed for eight city blocks in each direction. If any one path is blocked by a dead end, a cul de sac, or a park, it is not a true crossroad. The crossroad is the place to go to unblock your path. The wisdom of Hecate will be found there to help you choose the right direction in which to proceed. The strength of Ellegua lies at the crossroad. He is the remover of obstacles. An offering of twenty-one pennies and three candies left at the crossroad will prompt him to be kind and remove the roadblocks in your life.

Crystals

RULER: Earth Mother
TYPE: minerals
MAGICKAL FORM: raw, polished

All forms of crystals have healing powers. Some witches use them as wands or daggers. *Crystal balls* are used for scrying or divining the future. Spirits and ascended astral masters can be channeled through crystals. They bring energy and renewal to the physical and astral body. When placed on altars, they magnify the intention of all other tools vibrating there. Be sure to clean crystals in saltwater before use.

Cucumber

RULER: Venus, Yemanja
TYPE: vegetable
MAGICKAL FORM: seed, oil, flesh

Place round cucumber slices over the eyes to alleviate stress. Dab the oil on the temples to calm the mind. Eat cucumber slices on a new moon to energize and renew the physical and spiritual body. Rub into white candles and burn or add to floor wash to bless the home. Dry cucumber seeds and add to love potions to increase sexual allure. Offer whole cucumbers to the ocean with prayers for inner beauty to be reflected on the outside.

Cumin

RULER: Mars
TYPE: spice
MAGICKAL FORM: powder, seed

Sprinkle cumin in the shoes of a wandering lover to make him or her stop cheating and stay at home. You can also place the seeds under the pillow to keep his or her mind off another person. Keep the seeds in a wallet or purse to prevent theft. Sprinkle or burn the powder around the home to ward off thieves.

Curry

RULER: Saraswati
TYPE: spice
MAGICKAL FORM: powder

This hot spicy seasoning is sacred to the goddess of intelligence. Eat some to open the mind and dust the hands for success in higher education. Serve with rice to bless newlyweds. Add to fish to bring fertility. Dust the hands and feet for serious protection from evil.

Cyclamen

RULER: Venus
TYPE: flower
MAGICKAL FORM: flower, oil

This scent eases pain, especially the pain of childbirth. Rub the oil into white candles for successful conception and a safe term. Rub into red candles for an easy delivery, or into yellow candles to bless mother and newborn child.

Cypress

RULER: Saturn, Hecate
TYPE: tree
MAGICKAL FORM: oil, leaves

Burn the leaves or rub oil into purple candles to receive the wisdom of the goddess. Rub oil into black candles to reverse a curse sent by an enemy. If aging gracefully troubles you, place a fresh sprig of cypress on your altar to slow down the aging process and help you become reconciled to your age.

Daffodil

RULER: Venus
TYPE: plant
MAGICKAL FORM: fresh or dried flowers

Sprinkle dried petals or place fresh flowers on an altar to attract friendly spirits. Keep in the house or garden to cheer you up. Add to bathwater to increase your luck and bring new people into your life. Mix with rose petals and place around a photo of a lover you want to return to you.

Daisy

RULER: Venus
TYPE: flower
MAGICKAL FORM: petals

A flower of friendship and courtship, the daisy is used to open up social or romantic opportunity. Add the petals to bathwater on Wednesdays to draw new friends. Place whole flowers on a love altar with pink candles to attract romantic possibilities. The daisy is not a flower of passion and it is a great choice for young men and women who prefer a long courtship to sexual promiscuity. The daisy is the emotional and intellectual "getting to know you" flower.

Damiana

RULER: Venus, Mars
TYPE: herb
MAGICKAL FORM: extract, dried

An aphrodisiac, damiana is often added to potions to enhance passion. Add the extract to red wine or brew the herb into a tea. Drink hot or iced to increase sexual stamina. To increase sex appeal, add damiana herb or extract to incense or oil recipes and burn, wear as a perfume, or rub into red candles.

Dandelion

RULER: Leo
TYPE: flower
MAGICKAL FORM: tea, fresh flower

Place fresh or dried dandelion flowers under the pillow or

sew into a special dream pillow to enhance dream activity. Brew and drink the tea on a full moon to increase psychic awareness and increase the ability to interpret dreams. Dandelion tea is also used in healing rituals. Add the fresh bitter flowers to salad greens to increase physical strength.

Date

RULER: Saturn, Venus
TYPE: fruit
MAGICKAL FORM: dried, fresh

One of the strongest psychic cleansers, dates rid the body of negativity and can also ward off bad vibes. Dates are believed to decimate enemies and obstacles. They also carry a vibration of love. Eat dates rolled in powdered sugar to remove blocks in your love life and draw new and exciting romantic possibilities.

Datura

RULER: Saturn, Hecate
TYPE: plant
MAGICKAL FORM: seeds, leaves

One of the most sacred herbs, datura is also highly poisonous and should be handled with gloves, as it can cause skin irritation. It is also known as jimson weed, stinkweed, devil's apple, yerba del diablo, and ghost flower. Sprinkle around a house you think is haunted to drive away evil or troubled spirits. Mix with beech bark and sprinkle on an altar or Ouija board to communicate with friendly ghosts. Add to flying ointments to increase psychic vision. Datura is also used for cursing enemies. Place the seeds in a bowl on top of something belonging to the person you want to affect. Hide the bowl in a dark place. This is very baneful magick but will not harm the person unless they are actively trying to harm you.

Deerstongue

RULER: Venus
TYPE: herb
MAGICKAL FORM: oil, dried

This herb is the infamous "tongue of dog" and was so named because deer and dogs love to munch on the grass. Also known as wild vanilla grass, deerstongue is used in love spells to summon a gentle and true partner. It is favored by homosexuals but can be used by anyone seeking a companion. Prepare a bath with drops of the oil or dried herb. Add to love incense and sachets or rub the oil into red male or female figure candles to attract a potential mate.

Devil's Shoestring

RULER: Pan, Hecate
TYPE: plant
MAGICKAL FORM: root

Ward off evil with the tangled gnarled root of the devil's shoestring. Carry a piece of knotted root in your pocket for protection. Steep a quarter pound of the roots in water and then let cool. Use as a floor wash to protect a space and expel all evil from the premises.

Dill

RULER: Venus
TYPE: plant
MAGICKAL FORM: fresh, dried

Add dill, a favorite love ingredient, to any dish to spice up your love life. Feed to a tired partner to wake up his or her passions. Dill is also used for protection and healing. Chicken soup with dill is great for your health and well-being.

Dirt

RULER: earth spirits, Hecate
TYPE: soil
MAGICKAL FORM: gathered on dark, new, or full moon

In voodoo and Spanish magick, earth is one of the most powerful ingredients that can be added to a spell. Dirt from a crossroads is used to summon the goddess Hecate in her aspect of wise one and protector. It is also used to summon the Yoruban Ellegua, who helps clear the road and aids in important decision making. Use dirt from outside a cemetery to call the spirits of the dead. Add dirt from outside a bank for a powerful money spell when a loan is needed or the practitioner wants to get out of debt. Use dirt from outside a church to gain spiritual or political power and add dirt from outside a courthouse or law firm to potions aimed at legal success.

Dittany of Crete

RULER: Egyptian, Cretan and Minoan deities, Venus
TYPE: plant
MAGICKAL FORM: oil, herb

Use this very spiritual plant to clear the head of cobwebs and bring about enlightenment. The herb or oil is a sacred ingredient that summons the gods and goddesses of ancient Crete and Minoan pantheons.

Dogs

RULER: Hecate, Moon
TYPE: animal
MAGICKAL FORM: the bark

Canines are not only man's best friend but the goddess's as well. Witches who have dogs as familiars will always be fore-warned of danger. Any witch hearing the barking of a dog should be aware that a message from the lunar goddess is on its way. To dream of a dog brings good fortune.

Dogwood

RULER: Diana
TYPE: tree
MAGICKAL FORM: sap, branch, leaf, flower

Sit under a dogwood tree and make a wish for adventure. Add leaves to love sachets to promote loyalty and fidelity.

Carry the branch or bark to draw trustworthy people into your life. To help pets get along, take a hair clipping from each one and add to a jar of sugar water with dogwood sap. Shake the bottle daily until the animals stop fighting.

Doorknobs

RULER: Ellegua, Mercury
TYPE: brass, copper, silver
MAGICKAL FORM: attached or unattached to a door

Gaining access is always an issue in spellcraft. Doorknobs often provide an innocuous and subtle way to influence another person. Doorknobs can also be used in personal rituals to open metaphorical doors. Rub a small dab of coconut oil into a doorknob and as you turn it, make a wish concerning something or someone you wish to access. Carry a doorknob with you when you feel that too many doors are closed in your life. Continue to carry until you feel things opening up.

Dragons

RULER: Air, Fire, Water, Earth
TYPE: mythical beast
MAGICKAL FORM: statuary, visualization

Slaying a dragon in a dream or vision quest symbolizes overcoming obstacles or evil. In Eastern mythology, the creature is a symbol of immortality and happiness. Dragons or griffins placed over archways or facing doors serve as guardians protecting a dwelling from spiritual harm. Dragon tattoos protect and empower the wearer. The dragon is a popular image in pagan and magickal art. Summon a dragon in a magick circle when you need help in guarding something important to you.

Dragonsblood

RULER: Sun
TYPE: resin from palm tree
MAGICKAL FORM: chunks, powder

When your nerves are shot, add sea salt and dragonsblood powder to a bath to create peace and calm. Sprinkle or burn the powder in a dwelling to protect the inhabitants. Burn a combination of frankincense, myrrh, and dragonsblood powders for serious psychic protection. Mix dragonsblood powder with alcohol and gum arabic to create a powerful ink for the creation of magickal talismans.

E

East

RULER: air, Archangel Raphael
TYPE: direction
MAGICKAL FORM: incense

Wiccan altars traditionally face the east. To draw the magick circle, begin and end in the east. Sylphs and fairies rule this quadrant. Sleeping with your head facing east energizes the body and mind.

Echinacea

RULER: Sun, Mars
TYPE: herb
MAGICKAL FORM: powder, tincture, leaves, root

Take internally or sprinkle externally to heal emotional wounds and strengthen resolve. This herb protects warriors and brings longevity.

Egg

RULER: fertility goddesses, Moon
TYPE: food
MAGICKAL FORM: whole

Eat a whole salted hard-boiled egg on the new moon for rejuvenation and rebirth. Eggs also make great psychic cleansers, as they absorb negative energy. Add a whole raw egg to the bath with sea salt and soak for ten minutes to remove bad vibes. Carefully roll the egg around your body without breaking it. When you finish the bath, let the water drain and remove the egg. Smash it inside a paper bag and then dispose of it outside the house. To cleanse a house of bad energy, place nine whole raw eggs around the home. After nine days, remove the eggs and dispose of them. Use crushed and pulverized eggshells as chalk to draw magickal seals. They are also added to incense blends to remove jinxes.

Eggplant

RULER: Jupiter, Oya
TYPE: vegetable
MAGICKAL FORM: dark purple, white

To gain wisdom and insight, especially for making an important decision, carve your name into an eggplant while meditating upon your dilemma. Slice and cook the eggplant and eat one quarter of it. Within four days, you will gain insight into, or help with, your decision. Eat *purple eggplant* to gain power and emotional strength; they will also bring out the warrior spirit in you. Consume *white eggplant* for purification and protection.

Elder

RULER: mother goddesses
TYPE: tree
MAGICKAL FORM: branch, leaves, berries

A wand made of an elder branch prevents psychic attack. It is also believed that spirits live in the elder and using it in rituals will stir up paranormal activity. Scatter the leaves around an altar to ward off evil. Place the berries in a sleep pillow to cure insomnia. Use elderberries in love spells to prevent cheating.

Elecampane

RULER: Mercury
TYPE: plant
MAGICKAL FORM: leaves, flower

Sprinkle flowers or dried leaves over a Ouija board to increase its powers and to attract beneficial spirits. Elecampane is a strong communication herb and creates good vibes between humans as well. Add to love formulas to bring happiness and understanding. This is the best herb to carry when you seem to attract lovers you actually have nothing in common with outside the bedroom. Mix with goldenseal to draw a kindred soul and add a pinch of mustard seed powder to make sure sexual passion will flourish as well.

Elemental

RULER: Hecate
TYPE: spirit
MAGICKAL FORM: various apparitions

Witches perform rituals to conjure elemental spirits. These spirits help them accomplish certain goals. When creating an elemental, it is important to create both a birth and a death date for the spirit. There must also be a designated vessel to house it in. Quartz crystals or bottles with corked tops make excellent housing for elemental spirits.

Elements

RULER: east, south, west, north
TYPE: force or energy
MAGICKAL FORM: air, fire, water, earth

Casting a ritual circle involves invoking the elements or spirits of the four directions. Face each direction as the priest or priestess calls down the protective energies of each directional element to guard the circle. The elements are also used to bless, purify, and consecrate any magickal tool as well as any member of the circle. To do this, sprinkle salt and pass incense smoke around the object or person to be blessed. Hold up the light of a candle flame and pass it around the person or object. Finally sprinkle water on whatever or whoever is to be consecrated.

Elephant

RULER: Ganesh
TYPE: animal
MAGICKAL FORM: statuary

This great beast is sacred to the Hindu god Ganesh, lord of the obstacles. Keep *white elephant* statues on your altar to remove blocks in your path. *Green elephant* statues draw wealth. All elephant statues should display the elephant's trunk held up for good luck.

Elm

RULER: Odin, Woden
TYPE: tree
MAGICKAL FORM: bark, branch, leaves

Carry a consecrated elm wand to see elves and fairies. It is best to choose a fallen branch but if you prune one, make sure the tree is not damaged and leave some coins as an offering under the tree. The branches are also said to protect against lightning. Burn the leaves or bark to increase psychic vision and intuition.

Emerald

RULER: Venus
TYPE: mineral
MAGICKAL FORM: raw, polished

This precious gemstone draws love and admiration. It is the birthstone of Taurus and attracts sensual pleasure and wealth. When used in healing rituals, emeralds cure female reproductive problems and help with hormonal imbalance. This mineral also improves the eyesight and brings the psychic sight.

Endive

RULER: Mars
TYPE: vegetable
MAGICKAL FORM: raw, cooked

Eat this vegetable raw to increase your prosperity. Steam a whole endive and eat with a partner to increase sexual pleasure.

Eucalyptus

RULER: Mars
TYPE: plant
MAGICKAL FORM: leaf, essential oil

Use this plant for healing, cleansing, protection, and greater physical energy. Put a leaf or drops of oil in a bowl of water and place in a room to ward off illness. Rub the oil into red candles to gain strength and endurance. The scent also stimulates brain cells and increases concentration.

Evening Primrose

RULER: Venus
TYPE: plant
MAGICKAL FORM: oil

Add drops to bathwater or anoint pulse points to heal female problems and prevent depression and mental illness. Also add drops to beauty spells. Primrose flowers grown in a garden protect children.

Eyebright

RULER: Mercury, Asclepious
TYPE: plant
MAGICKAL FORM: dried leaves

The leaves are used medicinally to heal eye problems. Eyebright can also enhance the third eye or psychic sight. Drink the tea or anoint the middle of the brow with drops of cooled tea. It is also good for memory and revealing secrets.

Eye of Newt

RULER: Hecate
TYPE: plant
MAGICKAL FORM: berries

There are different theories on this Shakespearean ingredient. Some say it is the real eye of a salamander or small fish. Others argue that eye of newt is actually a slang name for a marsh berry and is associated with the red berries of the belladonna (deadly nightshade) plant. It is a poisonous narcotic and used to prepare heart medication. The plant grows freely like a weed and is easily obtained. Crush the berries and add to incense or ointments to foretell the future. Sprinkle berries outside the home to ward off devils.

Eyes

RULER: Horus
TYPE: talisman
MAGICKAL FORM: metal, ceramic, paper, or wax talisman

Many cultures use the symbol of the eye and believe it will watch over and protect them. In Greece and Turkey, *blue ceramic eyes* are worn or hung over doorways to ward off the evil eye. The eye is sometimes worn at the back of the neck to "watch their backs." The *Egyptian eye of Horus* is worn or carved into candles or drawn on parchment seals for protection and guidance. Eat *fish eyes* for vision and protection.

Feather

RULER: Maat, spirits of air
TYPE: animal part
MAGICKAL FORM: various colors and feather types

Carry any feather for swift communications. Turkey feathers bring luck and protection. Add *pigeon* or *dove feathers* to love ouanga bags to bring long-lasting love. Place *red feathers* on an altar to call Maat, the Egyptian goddess of judgment. Call her to bring about justice or karma in a situation.

Fennel

RULER: Mercury, Dionysus
TYPE: vegetable
MAGICKAL FORM: seed, stalk

Sprinkle the seeds around a phone or computer to bring business through communication. Eat fennel to inspire more creative ideas for money making. Ancient Greeks used fennel stalks to construct the sacred thyrsus, or rod of Dionysus, which was used in fertility rites. Eat whole stalks and seeds to improve chances of conception. Steep seeds in red wine to improve your sex life.

Fenugreek

RULER: Moon
TYPE: plant
MAGICKAL FORM: powder, seed

Sprinkle the seeds across the threshold of a business to draw clients. Use fenugreek powder in spells to protect nursing mothers and newborns. Dust orange candles with the powder and light them to energize a mother. Dust yellow candles and light them for a healthy child. Dust blue candles and light them to help correct an infant's sleep patterns.

Fern

RULER: Mercury
TYPE: plant
MAGICKAL FORM: whole plant, leaves, seed

Those who grow a fern inside or outside their home are

granted protection. A leaf hidden in a room will expose an evil sorcerer and prevent any magickal attack. When carried, the seeds are believed to make one "invisible." The seeds also bring luck to thieves or anyone needing stealth to accomplish a goal.

Feverfew

RULER: Mars
TYPE: plant
MAGICKAL FORM: dried

Carry feverfew to prevent winter colds and flu. Add to protection and healing spells to strengthen the aura and immune system.

Fig

RULER: fertility goddesses
TYPE: fruit
MAGICKAL FORM: fresh, dried, oil

The Bible speaks of figs as a food of healing, peace, prosperity, and happiness. In pagan lore they are a symbol of the fertility and sexuality of the Goddess. Eat fresh figs for health and to increase chances of getting pregnant. Offer them to the Goddess (under a tree or in a river) as a prayer for conception. Dried figs promote creativity and playfulness. Wear the oil for prosperity and good health.

Fir Balsam

RULER: Sun
TYPE: tree
MAGICKAL FORM: incense

Burn to cleanse a room of negative vibes. This is a wonderful incense for healing and strengthening the physical, emotional, and spiritual body. The scent opens the heart and increases endurance.

Fire

RULER: Mars, Vulcan, spirits of the south
TYPE: element
MAGICKAL FORM: candles

The element of fire represents the will, drive, and actions taken. It is associated with the quadrant of the south. Candle magick is one of the most powerful ways to activate the fire energy. Burning candles with requests written upon them will help manifest your own drive to take action and bring these desires into being. Paper talismans can also be burned to activate their power and provide motivation to apply your own energy toward achieving your goal.

Fish

RULER: Christ, Neptune, Venus, all ocean deities
TYPE: animal
MAGICKAL FORM: raw, cooked, flesh, eyes, skin, images

The eyes of a fish are particularly protective; eat them to invoke the magic. Cook and eat whole fish while visualizing protection. Draw fish images on parchment or formed out of metal to create talismans. Also eat fish for prosperity. A coin with a symbol of a fish makes a great talisman to carry for wealth. Use the skin of a fish in fertility magic.

Five-Finger Grass

RULER: Mars
TYPE: herb
MAGICKAL FORM: dried

Sprinkle around the premises inside and out for protection from thieves. Scatter some of this herb under the bed to dispel evil spirits and nightmares. Or carry some in a red ouanga bag in your pocket to gain power and influence over others. Five-finger grass is also known as cinquefoil.

Flax

RULER: Jupiter, Saturn
TYPE: plant
MAGICKAL FORM: seeds, oil

Grind the seeds and add to your diet to bring steady work. Add the oil to your bathwater to find a job. Sprinkle whole seeds in the four corners of a business or dwelling to attract prosperity. Flax is also used in healing rituals. Grind the seeds and sprinkle generously on food to increase endurance and stamina.

Floor Wash

RULER: household deities
TYPE: mop water in a bucket
MAGICKAL FORM: liquid (sometimes steeped in herbs)

Santeria, voodoo, and Wicca all use the ritual of washing down floors. The floor wash may include various ingredients depending on its purpose, the most common being lemon, drop of ammonia, crushed bay leaves, and salt, which are used for general household cleansings. There are washes for love, health, protection, success, and prosperity. The floor must be swept and mopped properly, cleaned of all dirt before the magical floor wash is administered.

Flour

RULER: Native American deities
TYPE: finely ground meal, grain
MAGICKAL FORM: white or whole wheat

Sprinkle flour around a new home or business to purify and bless it. Add a pinch of flour to the bathwater to remove negative vibes. Add flour to money-drawing recipes. Use *white flour* for purification and spiritual cleansing. *Whole-wheat flour* brings financial security.

Fluorite

RULER: Mercury
TYPE: mineral
MAGICKAL FORM: various colors

Pass this gemstone around the body to cleanse the aura.

Hold it to the forehead for increased clarity. Use *white fluorite* for healing and purification. *Yellow fluorite* improves the memory. *Purple fluorite* improves the psychic vision. Carry *blue fluorite* for protection and to cleanse and balance the emotions.

Flying, see Broom

Foxglove

RULER: Sun and Pluto
TYPE: plant
MAGICKAL FORM: leaves

Pharmaceutical companies make the heart medication Digitalis from purple foxglove. The plant is highly poisonous and this poison was fed to people during the Medieval inquisition for the "trials by ordeals" to discover whether or not certain individuals were witches. Do not ingest but rather grow in the garden to protect the household or add to witches bottles for serious protection.

Frangipani

RULER: Venus
TYPE: flower
MAGICKAL FORM: flower, oil

Wear this fragrance to attract friends, loyalty, adventure, and pleasure. Rub the scent into white or yellow candles on a Sunday for happiness. Use pink candles and burn on Fridays to master the art of flirting. Wear frangipani mixed with lotus and sandalwood to obtain knowledge of sexual secrets.

Frankincense

RULER: Sun
TYPE: plant resin
MAGICKAL FORM: beads, powder, oil

Burn frankincense to attract happiness and good health, also to purify a space and drive out evil. Wear the oil to attract good fortune and protection. Rub the oil on yellow or gold candles for success. Frankincense is also one of the best oils to work with in overcoming addictions.

Freesia

RULER: Iris
TYPE: flower
MAGICKAL FORM: fresh or dried flower, oil

This is the flower of tenderness and belongs to the goddess who rules the rainbow. It is another reminder that there will always be calm after a storm. Wear this fragrance or keep the fresh flowers on your altar when you feel restless, anxious, or agitated. It not only alleviates fear and worry but also calms obsessive behavior. It is one of the best ingredients to heal a broken heart or combat worries over a difficult relationship or breakup.

Friday

RULER: Venus, Freya
TYPE: day of the week
MAGICKAL FORM: sunrise and the eighth, sixteenth, and twenty-fourth hours of the day

A god, goddess, or planet governs each day of the week. It is easy to spot the ruler of the day by its name. In the word *Friday*, we see the roots of the name of the Norse goddess Freya. In the romance languages such as Italian or Spanish, this day of the week is called Viernes and is derived from the goddess Venus. Work magick for love, money, and health on Fridays. The hour of sunrise and every eight hours after that are also ruled by Venus, which makes these times of the day doubly blessed. These are the strongest four hours for conducting a ritual. Check your local newspaper, astrological calendar, or almanac to determine your sunrise.

G

Galangal

RULER: Mars
TYPE: plant
MAGICKAL FORM: root, powder, oil

This is one of the best roots to break a bad habit, such as overeating or smoking. Chewing on galangal root curbs the appetite and tones down nicotine cravings. Carry in the pocket into court to influence a jury. Rub the oil or sprinkle the powder onto purple candles to increase your power in any legal situation.

Galbanum

RULER: Sun
TYPE: gum resin
MAGICKAL FORM: oil, incense

One of the ingredients of the biblical holy incense burned in the temple of Solomon, galbanum is a sacred fragrance that lifts the soul to spiritual heights. Dab the oil on your body to ground and calm the spirit and bring religious insight. Burn incense for purification.

Gardenia

RULER: Moon
TYPE: flower
MAGICKAL FORM: fresh or dried flowers, oil

The full fragrance of this flower invokes the power of the full moon. Float in water on an altar to increase your psychic awareness. Add drops of the oil to bathwater to increase your personal power and influence. The gardenia makes a strong love potion; use it to capture the attention and devotion of another. Dry the petals and grind into a powder. Rub into the skin before seeing the one you intend to influence or sprinkle the powder over a threshold that he or she is sure to walk across.

Garlic

RULER: Hecate, Mars
TYPE: plant
MAGICKAL FORM: garlands, whole bulbs, raw and roasted

This plant is highly valued for its medicinal properties and ability to drive away evil. Hang garlands of garlic above doorways to expel illness and demons, or hang in kitchens to prevent accidents. Roman soldiers ate garlic cloves to protect themselves in battle. According to ancient Jewish and Arabic sources, eating garlic increases the sperm count.

Garnet

RULER: Sun, Saturn
TYPE: mineral
MAGICKAL FORM: raw, polished

The stone of passion and power, garnet increases social standing and sexual prowess. It is one of the best gems to wear when looking for a wealthy spouse or climbing the ladder to business success. It carries a good vibration that quickly helps develop trust and intimacy with others.

Garter (or Girdle)

RULER: Hecate, Venus
TYPE: ritual garment
MAGICKAL FORM: red (or red and black)

Worn on the thigh of a witch queen or high priestess after she has had three or more groups branch off her original coven. It is a symbol of power in the craft and represents great achievement in spreading the word of the Goddess. The red garter is worn on sabbats and full moons. Garters are good for love magick. Dust the garter with orris powder and wear high on the right thigh to draw out a shy lover.

Geranium

RULER: Moon
TYPE: flower
MAGICKAL FORM: flower, oil

This positive and affirming flower is best for increasing self-confidence and healing a blow to the ego. The geranium soothes a broken heart. Rub into white candles to help make a serious decision about whether to stay or leave a relationship.

Ginger

RULER: Mars, Sun
TYPE: spice
MAGICKAL FORM: powder or root, fresh or dried

Use this powerful root for energy, luck, healing, and sex magick. Carve your initials into a whole gingerroot and carve the name of the one you desire into another whole root. Bind the two roots together with a red cord to deepen the relationship and move it toward a firmer commitment. Place a whole gingerroot or ginger powder on top of a photograph of a person who needs healing. Add ginger to the bath to bring fast luck and eat on Tuesdays for added energy.

Ginkgo

RULER: Kwan-yin
TYPE: tree
MAGICKAL FORM: nuts, fruit, extract

The "two-lobed silver apricot," or ginkgo biloba, is one of the oldest trees on the planet. It originated in China but now populates the world. Also known as Maidenhair, it is used to protect the virtue and chastity of young girls. Place a picture of the youth who needs guarding underneath the tree, or place a circle of ginkgo nuts around the photo. Place flowers from the male species upon an altar to help create order and strengthen character. Place flowers from the female species on an altar to gain attention and influence in the world. Eat the fruit or extract to bring tranquillity and a long life.

Ginseng

RULER: Mars
TYPE: plant
MAGICKAL FORM: root

In ancient China, ginseng was seen as a wonder drug or panacea and was used to cure many ailments. It is said to improve male sexual stamina. Sick people chew on the root to regain health. A healthy person chews on the root to increase vitality. Because it resembles the human form, the ginseng root makes an excellent healing poppet (or doll). Attach fingernail clippings or hair of the infirm to the root and then put it in a red cloth bag. Place the bag near the person needing healing.

Glitter (or Fairy Dust)

RULER: fairies
TYPE: decorative sparkles
MAGICKAL FORM: various colors

Use glitter, which is also called fairy dust, to adorn magick candles. It serves two purposes. The first is to outline a design or sigil carved into the candle. This serves as a visual reminder to the magician as the candle burns. It opens the door to the unconscious and aligns the will of the practitioner with the objective of the candle thus furthering chances for manifestation. The second purpose of glitter is to attract the attention of fairies or friendly spirits who will then come toward the candle and make a wish come true. You can also use glitter to decorate an altar or a paper talisman.

Gnocchi

RULER: Mercury
TYPE: pasta
MAGICKAL FORM: cooked

In Argentina there is a special ritual practiced by Italian immigrants. They eat gnocchi on the twenty-ninth day of the month to prevent poverty; and they believe it enables them to meet all their financial obligations of the coming month. To follow tradition, place some coins or a bill under the plate of gnocchi before you eat. After the meal, place this money in your pocket or purse as a money-drawing talisman.

God

RULER: divine masculine energy
TYPE: deity
MAGICKAL FORM: statuary, name

In pagan practice, god images are essential. Although they do not actually believe that the god is the statue or image, they do believe that the divine spirit may enter into the graven image and that the image will put him or her in touch with a specific aspect of the divine. God images vary from stone or metal statues to symbols in nature such as a pinecone. In Wicca, God is knowable, and outward representations help to connect to the god within. Chant the names of the god to increase your power.

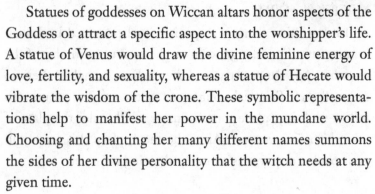

Goddess

RULER: divine feminine energy
TYPE: deity
MAGICKAL FORM: statuary, name

Statues of goddesses on Wiccan altars honor aspects of the Goddess or attract a specific aspect into the worshipper's life. A statue of Venus would draw the divine feminine energy of love, fertility, and sexuality, whereas a statue of Hecate would vibrate the wisdom of the crone. These symbolic representations help to manifest her power in the mundane world. Choosing and chanting her many different names summons the sides of her divine personality that the witch needs at any given time.

Gold

RULER: Apollo, all solar deities
TYPE: mineral
MAGICKAL FORM: solid, liquid

Modern-day alchemists ingest liquid gold, or aurum, with the belief that it will lengthen the life span and reveal secret wisdom. It is available as a tincture in homeopathic stores.

Choose the color gold as an altar cloth or candle to bring prosperity. Wear gold for protection, power, and to draw positive energy.

Goldenseal, *see* Turmeric

Gotu Kola, *see* Kola Nut

Gourd

RULER: Venus, Hecate
TYPE: fruit from the calabash tree
MAGICKAL FORM: dried

Leave a gourd under a tree as an offering to Hecate to remove bad karmic vibrations. This can only be done between the autumn equinox and Samhain (September 21 to October 31). Dried gourds used as drinking cups or chalices become sacred to Venus. A gourd cup shared and followed by a kiss will tie a knot of love.

Grains of Paradise

RULER: Jupiter
TYPE: grain
MAGICKAL FORM: seed

Burn the seeds for protection and to invoke spiritual evolvement. Carry the seeds in a green ouanga bag to draw wealth, good fortune, and gamblers' luck.

Grapefruit

RULER: Moon
TYPE: fruit
MAGICKAL FORM: skin, flesh

On a dark moon, peel the skin off the fruit in one whole piece and hang the skin above a doorway for serious protection. By the full moon, the skin should be completely dried. Remove it and grind to a fine powder. Sprinkle the dust outside your home (at doors and windows) to keep enemies away for good. Eat the flesh of the grapefruit to promote chastity and heal sexual hang-ups. When eaten during a waning moon (the full moon to new moon period), it can lift the spirits and reenergize the weary.

Grapes

RULER: Bacchus and his maenads, Moon
TYPE: fruit
MAGICKAL FORM: green, purple, red

This sacred fruit invokes "madness" or the frenzy of being possessed by the god. Eat some on a full moon to open your ability to channel divinity. Consume *green grapes* every day from new moon to full moon to increase your income. Eat *purple grapes* on dark and full moons to gain psychic sight and increase your power and influence. *Red grapes* promote love; feed a crush a cluster to summon playfulness and lust.

Green

RULER: Venus, Jupiter, Lakshmi
TYPE: color
MAGICKAL FORM: candles, cloth, glitter

The color of money (at least in the United States), green is the best color to work with to attract wealth. It is also the color of healing. Use green in fertility rites and to open channels for new love or to heal emotional problems.

Guarana

RULER: Mars
TYPE: herb
MAGICKAL FORM: powder

Mix in success powders and dust your hands and feet to accomplish tasks swiftly. Add to lust formulas to prolong sexual stamina. Guarana powder has high caffeine content. Ingest two gelatin capfuls to stay awake and alert for long periods of time.

Guava

RULER: Venus
TYPE: fruit
MAGICKAL FORM: fresh

Eat guava or rub the pulp into the skin to improve female orgasms. Offer the whole fruit to the sea on a full moon with a prayer to marry and/or conceive children. This fertility fruit also brings wealth and creativity when eaten on a regular basis.

ℋ

Hail

RULER: Freya
TYPE: element
MAGICKAL FORM: pellets

Ice fallen from the sky is very powerful for magick spells. Collect hail and use it in a spell to melt the heart of someone who is angry with you to bring forgiveness. The hail can also be used to soften the heart of a crush that isn't interested in you. After collecting the hail, write the name of the person on a piece of paper and place it in a bowl on the altar. Put the hail pellets on top of the paper. As the hail melts, so will his or her heart.

Hair

RULER: Aphrodite
TYPE: from the head or genitals
MAGICKAL FORM: lock, strand

Sympathetic magick requires a belonging, or a part of the subject, in order to affect said subject. Use hair in love spells to get a lover to return or to cause another to fall in love with you. Use your own hair in love spells, steeping it in a potion that the subject will walk across or ingest.

Hand

RULER: Fortuna
TYPE: image of outstretched palm
MAGICKAL FORM: flesh, metal, paper, or wax talisman

One of the most powerful symbols of luck, fate, and protection is called the hand of Fatima, or the hand of Fortune, or the Hamsa. It is a depiction of an open palm. This hand may be drawn on parchment and carried, shaped out of silver or gold and worn, or carved into candles and burned. It is invoked to change the course of one's fate, especially when going through a run of bad luck. The hand can turn one's fortune around for the better and protect the user from harm. The real *human hand* can also show one's fate by interpreting the lines within it. The *hand of glory* is a medieval talisman that is now very difficult to obtain: the hand of a thief must be cut off and pickled and embalmed. Another thief then carries it to protect himself from being caught.

Harpie

RULER: Cretan goddesses
TYPE: mythical creature
MAGICKAL FORM: vultures, harp players

In matriarchal times the harpies were angelic creatures who carried souls to heaven. After they were demonized by the patriarchy, they became vultures that snatched the souls out of bodies. Harpies are usually depicted as winged birds with female heads. Whether in their positive or negative manifestation, their appearance usually means that someone is about to die. A carrion feather on the altar invokes the dark side of the Harpie. A harp string invokes the positive side.

Hawthorn

RULER: Mars
TYPE: tree
MAGICKAL FORM: leaves, berries, extract

Carry the leaves for protection against sexual harassment. Add berries to fertility and happiness spells. Take the extract internally to promote mental clarity. Mix hawthorn with oak and ash leaves and carry into the woods to be able to see fairies.

Hazel

RULER: Artemis, Apollo
TYPE: tree
MAGICKAL FORM: branch, nut

One of the most powerful wands for divination. Use the branch of this tree for a dowsing stick to locate lost objects. Eat the nuts to draw love and wisdom into your life. Eat together with a lover to increase the length of the relationship.

Heal-All

RULER: Sun, Asclepios
TYPE: plant
MAGICKAL FORM: dried

Add the herb to baths for healing rituals. Heal-all (also called self-heal) is sacred to the goddess Panecea, who is said to cure all ailments and diseases. Sprinkle it around yellow candles or white figure candles and light on Sundays for healing.

Heart

RULER: Leo, Sun, Venus
TYPE: human organ
MAGICKAL FORM: image

In Mexican magic the powerful images of the *corazón*, or heart, are hung in churches and above altars. These images reflect suffering and redemption. In ancient Aztec rituals, real human hearts were offered to the gods. Modern Wiccans use this symbol to open the heart. Carve into red candles to attract love. Carve into white candles to heal a broken heart.

Hearts of Palm

RULER: Sun, Venus
TYPE: vegetable
MAGICKAL FORM: stalks

This is one of the most sumptuous of aphrodisiacs. Eat three hearts on Sundays or Fridays to increase your sexual allure and sexual stamina. To create a powerful love potion, add hearts of palm to salads and serve and eat with someone you have a crush on—or with a longtime partner to revitalize your sex life.

Heather

RULER: Hestia, Vesta
TYPE: flower
MAGICKAL FORM: dried or fresh flowers, oil

When worn or carried, this virginal flower wards off unwanted sexual advances. It essentially tones down the passions. Take a bath in heather flowers, preferably during the moon's waning phase, to help break sex addictions. Wear heather oil to bring a relationship back to a friendship. Add the flowers to a floor wash to bless the home. Sprinkle some around the workplace to calm down a tyrannical boss.

Heliotrope

RULER: Helios, Sun, Apollo
TYPE: flower
MAGICKAL FORM: flower, oil

This flower is sacred to all solar deities and is associated with homosexual mystery cults. It makes an excellent gay love formula. Add the flowers to the bathwater before you go out clubbing. Because of its connection with the sun, it is also used in invisibility spells. (The sun pulls a disappearing act every night after sunset.) Rub into a bloodstone and carry under a coat to become invisible. (This really works, so please watch out for the cars because they won't see you!) Heliotrope also brings things to light—especially thieves. Rub the oil into a yellow candle to reveal who stole something from you.

Hellebore

RULER: Hecate
TYPE: herb
MAGICKAL FORM: leaves

Historically, this is one of the most popular witches' herbs, but because it is poisonous, it will be difficult to purchase, and when found, it must be handled with caution. Sprinkle powdered leaves on shoes and carry in pockets to become invisible. A pinch of hellebore is added to flying ointments for psychic visions and to induce astral travel. The ointments are rubbed into pulse points in the skin, but anyone with allergies should not attempt this.

Hematite

RULER: Saturn
TYPE: mineral
MAGICKAL FORM: polished and magnetized gemstones

This stone deepens concentration and helps put you in touch with your physical and sensual body. It promotes trust and well-being and improves your balance. Use hematite stones with a magnetic charge (check out a good gem shop to find these) to align the energies of the body. They can alleviate muscle ache and tension and strengthen the immune system and circulation.

Hemlock

RULER: Aesculapius
TYPE: plant
MAGICKAL FORM: bark, tincture

The great philosopher Socrates ended his life by drinking hemlock. In his last discussion with his disciples he expressed his belief in the eternalness of the soul. Hemlock is an herb of transcendence. It is highly poisonous and should not be ingested. Witches add it to flying ointments to elevate the soul and astral-project into other planes.

Hemp

RULER: Saturn
TYPE: plant
MAGICKAL FORM: seeds, leaves

Cannabis or marijuana use and cultivation apparently dates from 2737 B.C. The ancient Chinese, Hindus, Scythians, Thracians, and many others smoked ganja and hashish and ate the seeds for their hallucinatory effects. Hemp was and still is used to make clothing, medicine, ink, and fuel. For magick, sprinkle hemp seeds around love altars. Mix the buds into flying ointments or incenses and burn to gain psychic sight.

Henbane

RULER: Apollo
TYPE: plant
MAGICKAL FORM: dried

The oracle at Delphi (1400 B.C.) was the most important ancient Greek shrine. Priestesses who inhaled the smoke of burning henbane supposedly obtained the power of prophecy. The dried herb is still added to witches' flying incense to give priestesses visions. It can also be rubbed on the body in love spells to intoxicate another with love. Henbane has healing properties and is used in homeopathic medicines. But the plant is highly poisonous and great care should be taken when using it. Because it is so toxic, it is also used during dark moons to vex enemies and added to witches' bottles of protection to ward off evil.

Henna

RULER: Lakshmi
TYPE: plant
MAGICKAL FORM: powder

During the Inquisition, women with red hair or women caught using henna were burned at the stake. Its magickal powers are legendary. Stain the hands with henna for luck and protection. Stain the hair with henna to increase your psychic powers.

Herring

RULER: Yemanja, sea goddesses
TYPE: fish
MAGICKAL FORM: whole

According to legend, mermaids are actually nothing more than a shape-shifting school of herring; these small fish bond together in schools to form these mythological sea maidens. Herring hold the treasures and mysteries of the sea. Eat herring to increase your wealth, wisdom, and imagination. Always eat the head first.

Hexagram

RULER: Solomon
TYPE: six-pointed star
MAGICKAL FORM: metal or paper talisman

The two interlocking triangles that make up this star represent "as above, so below." The triangle pointing upward symbolizes the prayer or request sent to the heavens. The triangle pointing downward represents the magick that will manifest on the earth plane. The hexagram can be drawn to invoke planetary assistance. Saturn, Jupiter, Mars, Sun, Venus, Mercury, and the Moon each have their own hexagrams. It is traditional to carve the appropriate hexagram on the top of a candle when working with a planetary energy to ensure that the magick will manifest on the earth plane. The hexagrams are also drawn on the flip side of paper talismans. Magicians wear metal hexagrams for protection.

Hibiscus

RULER: Venus
TYPE: plant
MAGICKAL FORM: dried flowers

Drink the tea to increase energy and lift the spirits. Pour a cup of the tea into the bathwater to calm the nerves and alleviate worry and depression. Add to formulas for power, lust, and attraction.

Hickory

RULER: Jupiter
TYPE: tree
MAGICKAL FORM: smoke

Burn the bark for luck and to dispel evil. It lends a calming and protective spirit to all that inhale the smoke. It also opens the heart and eating hickory-smoked food will improve the love and family life.

Holly

RULER: Sun
TYPE: plant
MAGICKAL FORM: wreaths, berries, leaves

A Christian myth says that the blood of Christ formed the red berries of the holly. Carry its berries in your pocket for protection. The wreaths are very popular around Christmas and winter solstice time; they are brought in to bless and protect the house. Holly tames wild beasts and wards off storms and bad weather. Since it is a masculine herb, it brings good luck to men.

Honey

RULER: Oshun, bee goddess
TYPE: food
MAGICKAL FORM: any type

Use this sweet and sticky substance to attract good fortune, fertility, and love. For wealth, create an altar with coins drizzled with honey. For a conception spell, cover a pumpkin with honey and offer to a river. For love, bathe in warm water and honey. This is also a favorite offering for the love goddesses. An assassination attempt was once made on the African love goddess, Oshun. The plot was to poison her with honey. In remembrance of this, always taste the honey first before offering libations to any goddess.

Honeydew

RULER: Yemanja, Venus
TYPE: fruit
MAGICKAL FORM: whole, sliced

On a full moon, hold a whole honeydew in your arms and press to your heart while making a love wish. Eat half and offer half to the goddess by leaving at the ocean or beneath a tree. By the next full moon, your wish will come true. To save a troubled marriage, open a honeydew by slicing off a thin section of the top and remove the seeds. Stuff with allspice berries, whole almonds, coconut flakes, camphor shavings, cumin, and jasmine flowers. Crown the honeydew by scooping meringue on the top and pink and white sprinkles. Obtain seven white candles and carve the names of the couple into the sides of the candles. Use the honeydew as a candleholder by securing a candle into the top and letting it burn to completion. Repeat for seven days and then place the honeydew outside and say a prayer in your own words concerning the marriage.

Honeysuckle

RULER: angels, Mercury
TYPE: plant
MAGICKAL FORM: flowers, oil

Use this flower to foster better communication and increase your creative energy. In the summer months, suck the nectar of the fresh flowers for inspiration. Add the oil to orange or yellow candles for creative brainstorming. Rub into green candles for new moneymaking ideas.

Hood

RULER: Hecate
TYPE: cloth covering for head
MAGICKAL FORM: hooded robe

Hood coverings are considered sacred in many religions. Wiccans use the hood for cloaking and concealment. During medieval times, the hooded robe was used to conceal one's identity when traveling to and from a coven meeting. If you were seen, you might be burned at the stake. In modern Wicca, the hood helps the witch filter out the mundane and go deep within to discover his or her magickal powers. If you do not have a hooded robe, use a shawl or any black soft fabric to cover the head during ritual. It will aid your concentration and focus on your spell.

Hops

RULER: Mars
TYPE: herb
MAGICKAL FORM: beer, dried cut leaves

This herb is used in the brewing of beer. It is highly protective and enhances psychic ability. Bathe in or drink beer for the benefits of hops. Sprinkle dried leaves around a space that needs purification. Also, rub the leaves into the forehead before doing any divinatory work.

Horehound

RULER: Hecate
TYPE: herb
MAGICKAL FORM: dried

Sprinkle this herb in a circle around you, your bed, or your home to call off the Hounds of Hell, the guardians of Hecate's realm and the watchdogs of the sacred mysteries. In psychological terms, these dogs are the gatekeepers of our own creative unconscious. Feeling blocked? Sprinkle a generous amount of loose horehound over your head and shake it to get unblocked. Remember that it is by journeying through the unconscious that we stumble into the psychic realm or the world where the dark mother keeps her occult teachings.

Horseradish

RULER: Mars
TYPE: plant
MAGICKAL FORM: whole or shredded root

One of the strongest ingredients for male virility, the horseradish root is in essence magickal Viagra. It is cultivated in the spring and difficult to find at any other time of the year. Women should lay the whole root on the belly and visualize either getting pregnant or being satisfied sexually. Men must hold the whole root to the genitals and visualize long-lasting erections. Perform these visualizations on a full moon. Eat both *white* and *red* shredded horseradish at any time of the year for protection.

Horseshoe

RULER: Epona, Jupiter
TYPE: metal
MAGICKAL FORM: crescent side up

Hang above a door to increase your luck. The horseshoe should always be kept with the crescent side up to catch good luck. Those of you who live below the equator should keep the horseshoe crescent-side down.

Horsetail

RULER: Venus
TYPE: plant
MAGICKAL FORM: stem, leaves

Horsetail was used in ancient fertility rites. Hang a dried

stem above the bed to increase chances of conception. Carry the dried leaves in your pocket at the racetrack to pick winners.

Huckleberry

RULER: Mercury
TYPE: plant
MAGICKAL FORM: leaves, berries

Carry or eat the berries for good luck and protection. Burn the dried leaves in the house and spread or fan the smoke around to get rid of trickster spirits and poltergeist activity.

Hyacinth

RULER: Hyacinthus, Apollo
TYPE: plant
MAGICKAL FORM: fresh flower, oil

The flower is sacred to gay men. Wear it to solve all problems of love. Place drops of the oil in a spray bottle filled with spring water and mist a room to lift heaviness and cure depression. Rubbing the oil on the belly in the early stages of pregnancy is believed to protect women later on during childbirth.

Hydrangea

RULER: Mercury
TYPE: plant
MAGICKAL FORM: dried or fresh flowers

Grow in a garden to protect the household from evil. Add

flowers to a floor wash or bath to break a hex. Sprinkle the cut flower petals around an area where something was stolen to reveal a thief.

Hyssop

RULER: Jupiter
TYPE: plant
MAGICKAL FORM: dried leaves, oil

The Bible calls hyssop the herb of forgiveness. It was used over six thousand years ago in guilt offerings. Hyssop is a serious karmic herb and can be used to heal the world of negativity. Sprinkle upon the earth for world peace. Bathe in hyssop leaves or oil to alleviate feelings of guilt. Since it is also a holy herb, you may drink hyssop as a tea to deepen your connection to the divine.

J

Ice

RULER: Freya
TYPE: frozen water
MAGICKAL FORM: ice cubes

Putting a dangerous situation or person "on ice" is a serious form of protection. Though it will not harm anyone, the ice will prevent them from interfering in your life or cause you harm. Write the name of a person (or situation) on a small piece of paper. Fold up the paper and place it in an ice cube tray (or small plastic container or freezer bag). Fill it with water and place it in the freezer. But do not remove or thaw it until you feel the danger has passed. This old spell is highly effective. Ice cubes can also be used in love spells. Freeze water with drops of almond, orange, and lemon extract and add the cubes to a drink. Serve to a reluctant or shy partner.

Incense

RULER: spirits of air and the east
TYPE: smoke
MAGICKAL FORM: stick, cone, loose

The burning of incense to purify a temple or devotee is one of the oldest forms of spiritual practice. In essence, the smoke is offered as a pleasing supplication to the gods. Assigned to the element of air because of the smoke, incense also contains the elements of fire and earth. As air, it influences the mind and  thought. Through fire, it affects the will and actions. Through earth, it can bring about physical change. Although incense is most commonly used for purification, it can be burned to complement and advance the results of any magickal request.

Indian Head

RULER: Great Spirit
TYPE: image
MAGICKAL FORM: on a coin or talisman

Coins that depict an Indian head, such as the Indian-head

nickel, make wonderful prosperity talismans. Meditating on the image can bring on feelings of security and well-being. The Indian head represents understanding and respect of the land. Creating this alignment with the earth blesses the user with its benefits. The Indian head makes an excellent talisman of prosperity for farmers, gardeners, landscapers, or anyone who works off the land.

Ink

RULER: Mercury
TYPE: instrument of writing
MAGICKAL FORM: wet

Magickal inks are made in different colors using vegetable dyes, gum resins, and plant oil extracts. To make paper seals or talismans you should use a consecrated ink, which is created by adding drops of magickal ingredients to already prepared liquid ink. For example, a drop of musk oil added to *red ink* will enhance the powers of a love seal. Add finely ground frankincense to *green ink* to create a money seal.

Iris

RULER: Iris, the rainbow goddess
TYPE: plant
MAGICKAL FORM: fresh flowers

Place this flower on a healing or love altar to calm fears. Add to bathwater to overcome anger toward a spouse. The Iris promotes domestic bliss and stimulates creative energy when kept in the home.

Irish Moss

RULER: Jupiter
TYPE: plant
MAGICKAL FORM: fronds, moss

Also called carrageenan. The dried fronds should be added to money potions to bring long-lasting financial stability. Burn as incense to reduce anxiety and clear the mind. Irish moss is one of the best grounding ingredients and should literally be walked upon in bare feet to get your head out of the clouds and bring you back to realistic thinking. Add to bathwater for luck or beauty rituals.

Iron Filings

RULER: Vulcan, Saturn, Earth
TYPE: metal
MAGICKAL FORM: magnetic powdered iron shavings

You will need to visit a proper occult shop or botanica to obtain iron filings for creating a magnetic pull in your magick and draw down physical results. Add a sprinkle to the bottom of a glass or candleholder to add extra charge. Or sprinkle some into an ouanga bag filled with herbs. Iron filings are most used to complement love spells designed to attract someone.

Ivy

RULER: Bacchus
TYPE: plant
MAGICKAL FORM: leaves

Growing ivy brings good luck and protection to a property. It is a feminine plant that complements the masculine plant holly. Entwine together and place on an altar for love or fertility magick. Women should carry ivy for good luck. Add *poison ivy* to witches' bottles of protection but be careful not to touch it with your bare hands or expose it to any part of your skin.

Jack-o'-Lantern

RULER: spirits of the dead
TYPE: vegetable
MAGICKAL FORM: carved

Pumpkins are hallowed and carved for Halloween, or the night of the Feast of the Dead, to honor the spirits of the deceased. The white candles burned within them shed light for the journeys of these departed souls. The carved-out faces are scary in order to ward off malevolent spirits.

Jade

RULER: Buddha, Kwan-yin
TYPE: mineral
MAGICKAL FORM: polished or raw chunks

One of the most spiritual stones, jade teaches the balance of earth and spirit. It attracts wealth along with wisdom and is kept on prosperity altars or next to Buddha statues for good luck. Hold the stone to transmit calming vibrations into your aura. Jade is a stone of peace and harmony. It is also said to bring long life.

Jalup

RULER: Jupiter
TYPE: plant
MAGICKAL FORM: root, powder, oil

Also known as hi-john, or John the Conqueror, this root provides power, protection, and spiritual strength. For legal success, carry it in your pocket when you go to court. Add the powdered root to money spells. Rub the oil on purple candles for wealth and wisdom.

Jasmine

RULER: Lakshmi, Venus, Oshun
TYPE: plant
MAGICKAL FORM: fresh or dried flowers, oil

Brew and drink in a tea to induce psychic powers. Wear jasmine oil for power, seduction, and wealth. It is one of the best oils or flowers to use in ritual to bring prosperity into a relationship. Rub the oil into candles, or form a circle of the dried flowers around the candle. Use a white candle and meditate upon the flame to receive answers to spiritual questions. Use red to increase passion in your love life. Use green to draw money. To draw a rich spouse, place a jar of uncooked rice, dried jasmine flowers, and dried orange peel under the bed. Shake the jar each night and visualize yourself marrying well. Keep the jar under the bed and continue to shake until the marriage is consummated. Empty the contents of the jar into a moving body of water to ensure that love and prosperity continues to flow within the marriage.

Jasper

RULER: Venus, Mars
TYPE: mineral
MAGICKAL FORM: polished red, tiger, ocean

Wearing *ocean jasper* promotes relaxation, healing, peace, comfort, and compassion. The gemstone helps to end a relationship on a positive note. Place it on top of a photograph of a couple that needs help in letting go. Wear *tiger* or *red jasper* or place it in the work area to promote clear thinking and organization.

Jet

RULER: Moon, Hecate
TYPE: mineral
MAGICKAL FORM: beads

The high priestess wears a necklace of beads of amber and jet. The jet symbolizes her power and is worn to successfully draw down the goddess into the priestess. Jet relaxes the wearer and increases intuition. It is a very protective mineral and elevates the wearer to new spiritual heights. Wear it or hold one when you desire to channel divine energy. It helps the ego to move out of the way and opens the door to the unconscious.

Jezebel Root

RULER: Astarte
TYPE: plant
MAGICKAL FORM: whole root

This plant was named after the infamous queen who defended goddess worship in ancient Israel. Jezebel was killed and her body was thrown to the dogs. The Jezebel root is traditionally used to destroy enemies. Carve the name of your foe into the root and throw it in a body of water to defeat him or her. Carry the root to seduce men; it is a favorite money talisman for prostitutes.

Jicama

RULER: Jupiter
TYPE: legume
MAGICKAL FORM: raw, cooked

Eat this yam bean, or Mexican turnip, to heighten creative talents. It is especially effective for painters or visual artists. Eat jicama on full moons to promote sales of your work.

Job's Tears

RULER: Mercury, Jupiter
TYPE: grains
MAGICKAL FORM: loose or beaded pearls

Carry three pearls in your pocket when hunting for employment. Wear a strand around the wrist or neck for job success and promotion. Add to money charms and ouangas to increase your earning potential.

Juniper

RULER: Sun
TYPE: tree
MAGICKAL FORM: incense, fresh sprigs, berries, oil

Brew the berries into a tea and drink it to increase sexual stamina. Crush dried berries to release their scent and add to love potions to attract a man. Hang a sprig of fresh juniper in the home to drive away evil. Brush down the body with a bundle of sprigs to remove illness and place drops of oil in a bowl of water to promote healing in a sick room. Burn juniper for purification and good health. Gin (which is made from juniper) can be sprinkled across a threshold to guard against theft.

Kava Kava

RULER: Saturn
TYPE: herb
MAGICKAL FORM: tea, dried

Brew and drink small amounts of kava tea to increase psychic awareness. Sprinkle the dried herb across thresholds and windows for protection. Also, carry the herb in your pocket to keep harm from coming your way.

Ketchup

RULER: Venus
TYPE: condiment
MAGICKAL FORM: drawn in the shape of a pentagram

To flavor with love, use ketchup on foods. Squeeze it out of the bottle in the shape of a pentagram, the five-pointed star witches use to summon and dismiss energy. Draw the invoking pentagram beginning at the top point of the star and continue down to the left bottom. Then go diagonal to the right side, across to the left side, diagonal to the bottom right, and up again to the top point to complete the star. Visualize someone you want to attract in romantic relationship as you spread the ketchup. Continue to visualize or even call out this person's name as you eat it.

Key

RULER: Saturn
TYPE: metal
MAGICKAL FORM: old-fashioned

Wearing an old-fashioned key will unlock spiritual doors. Perform spells with identical keys, which are then worn by lovers to protect their relationship from infiltration. A key given to a lover who is going far away will keep you in his or her heart.

Kiwi

RULER: Venus
TYPE: fruit
MAGICKAL FORM: flesh

This exotic fruit draws love and material grounding. Eat kiwi to obtain both money and sex. It's a perfect fruit for those in the sex industry. Eat on Fridays to increase business.

Knot

RULER: Saturn
TYPE: a fastening created by looping and tying
MAGICKAL FORM: red cord, black shoelace

Witches practice knot magick, using either red or black cord or string, for a variety of reasons. Tie seven knots and make seven wishes concerning love. Then carry the knotted string in your breast pocket or near the heart as a talisman to make the wishes come true. Tie two figure candles with red cord to bind a couple together. Nine knots tied in black cord around a black figure candle will bind someone who wishes you harmed. Tie three knots in a shoelace and burn it. Then sprinkle the ashes behind you to confuse someone and throw him off your trail.

Knotgrass

RULER: Saturn
TYPE: plant
MAGICKAL FORM: dried

Use this plant to hex an enemy. Stuff some inside a black voodoo doll and bury it at midnight on a dark moon.

Kola Nut

RULER: Mercury
TYPE: plant
MAGICKAL FORM: nut, extract

Carry the nut as a talisman to jog your memory. Students should keep some in their pockets and rub some between their hands while studying for and taking tests. Place the liquid extract underneath your tongue to improve your memory. It works wonders for actors who need to memorize their lines.

Kunzite

RULER: Venus
TYPE: mineral
MAGICKAL FORM: unpolished or polished gemstone

Carry kunzite to calm your spirit and repel disruptive influences. The stone dispels loneliness and attracts caring friends. It also promotes self-love and self-discipline. It's a great stone to wear when you are being too hard on yourself.

L

Labdanum

RULER: Apollo
TYPE: resin
MAGICKAL FORM: oil

This thick dark oil is holy in the Middle East. Burn it for purification or wear some to channel divine energy. It is the oil of prophets and a small dab rubbed into the third eye brings clear visions of the future.

Lady's Mantle

RULER: Venus
TYPE: plant
MAGICKAL FORM: leaves

Add to love potions to catch a good husband or wife.

Lady's Slipper

RULER: Saturn, Hera
TYPE: plant
MAGICKAL FORM: leaf

Use for protection and to stop sexual harassment. Place in a sachet around the neck or sprinkle powdered leaves under carpeting at workplace.

Lamb

RULER: God
TYPE: meat
MAGICKAL FORM: roasted

The sacrificial, or Pascal, lamb was a powerful symbol at the Last Supper or Passover meal. In Christianity it represents Christ, the Lamb of God who died for the sins of man. In Judaism, it represents the sacrifice made to spare the lives of the Jews. The blood of the lamb was spread on the doorposts to protect them from the last plague of Egypt, the smiting of the firstborn sons. Eat lamb for protection and to cleanse yourself of sin.

Lamp

RULER: gods and goddesses of wisdom
TYPE: Household appliance
MAGICKAL FORM: oil, electric

The magickal tool of the hermit, the lamp symbolizes enlightenment. Burn oil lamps and stare into the flame when you need to get in touch with your inner guides. Rub a dab of oil into a lightbulb to scent a room. Depending on the kind of oil you use, the lamp will then help light the way or inspire you with an idea to solve a problem in your life. Stand underneath a lamppost to re-create nostalgic moments and summon the happiness of the past.

Lapus Lazuli

RULER: Neptune, Venus, Isis
TYPE: mineral
MAGICKAL FORM: cut and polished or raw

The stone of truth, lapis heals karmic wounds and understands your true path in life. Wear it to prevent the repetition of mistakes and move your life forward in a positive way. Meditate on the stone to get in touch with spirit guides and receive messages. The darkest blue stones make the wearer more mysterious and attract love and openness.

Larkspur

RULER: Venus
TYPE: plant
MAGICKAL FORM: flowers

Add to bathwater for protection. Sprinkle around a place or person who seems to be possessed, as larkspur frightens away ghosts and devils.

Lavender

RULER: Venus
TYPE: plant
MAGICKAL FORM: flower, oil

Add it to other ingredients (such as rose and mint) to make a very powerful love attraction formula. Use lavender, rose, and lemon for love healing. Mix it with chamomile and drink as a tea to cure insomnia. Use lavender alone and add to bathwater to calm the spirits. Burn dried lavender flowers with the herb rue for protection rituals.

Lead

RULER: Saturn, Vulcan
TYPE: mineral
MAGICKAL FORM: solid balls

Lead is toxic and very dangerous, especially for children. It is recommended that pewter be substituted for these rituals. In Germany on Silvester (New Year's Eve), small lead balls are heated on a spoon until they liquefy and then dropped into cold water, where they form shapes. These shapes are read and interpreted as signs for what the new year will hold. The lead shape is then carried throughout the year for good luck. In Turkey, lead is used to find out the cause of negative energy and also to remove it from a person. The afflicted individual sits in a chair and a tablecloth is held by two persons over the head of the one seated. A pot is held over the tablecloth. Lead is then heated by the wise woman and spilled into the cold pot. The woman reads the images formed to determine what is wrong. The lead pouring over the head is also believed to remove any evil within the afflicted.

Leeks

RULER: Moon
TYPE: vegetable
MAGICKAL FORM: steamed stalks

Used for exorcism rites in ancient Rome, dried leeks should be hung above a door to ward off evil. Eat them steamed for purification and protection from enemies. Leeks will also strengthen and prepare you for battle. Eat before any challenging spiritual or physical encounter.

Lemon

RULER: Moon
TYPE: fruit
MAGICKAL FORM: fresh fruit, dried peel, pulp, juice, oil

Use lemon, which is sacred to the moon, for pu-

rification and love. To purify, mix lemon with salt and scrub the skin or add to bathwater and soak. For love spells, add sugar to lemon juice and drink it, giving some as well to the one you desire. To solve love problems, burn white figure candles rubbed with lemon oil or extract. Cleopatra used lemon wedges to prevent wrinkles. It can also be added to anti-aging and beauty spells.

Lemongrass

RULER: Mercury
TYPE: plant
MAGICKAL FORM: dried and cut stalks, oil

A favorite spice of transvestites, lemongrass is the gender bender of herbs. Add to foods to open up your sensuality and create more playfulness and exploration of your sexuality. Wear the oil to bring forth the anima or animus.

Lemon Verbena

RULER: Sun
TYPE: herb
MAGICKAL FORM: dried, oil

Prepare a magickal bath or floor wash with lemon verbena to purify yourself and the room before ritual. Used alone, it cleanses and creates sacred space. Add it to love ingredients or money spells to remove obstacles and speed up the results.

Lettuce

RULER: Jupiter, Moon
TYPE: vegetable
MAGICKAL FORM: whole head, leaves

Eat the *dark-leafed* and *round* varieties on full moons for abundance. *Iceberg lettuce* is too lightweight to attract money but can calm the nerves or decrease financial worries. *Red-leaf lettuce* will give you energy to find a good job and push harder for getting ahead. It's a great choice for beating out the competition.

Libation

RULER: various gods and goddesses
TYPE: liquid
MAGICKAL FORM: wine, juice

The pouring off of liquid from a chalice into the ground is called a libation. Witches libate at the end of their rituals and it is common to say a prayer of thanks while libating. In a sense, it is like a toast: the glass is held high and praise is given to a particular god or goddess who has done something good for the libator. It is also common to ask or wish for something as a libation is poured.

Licorice, see Anise

Life Everlasting

RULER: Sun
TYPE: plant
MAGICKAL FORM: dried flowers

Add life everlasting, a heal-all herb, to any health spell to promote well-being. Bathe in the flowers for rejuvenation. Drink the tea on every new moon to lengthen your life.

Lightning

RULER: Jupiter, Zeus, Thor
TYPE: occurrence in nature
MAGICKAL FORM: rain

Rain collected from a lightning storm contains very powerful and magnetic energy that's used for magick. Add to bathwater or sprinkle over your head to increase your charisma. *Winter* storm water will enhance your endurance and make you a formidable foe in business or politics. *Spring* storm water increases your sensuality and can attract a powerful new love. *Summer* storm water creates personal magnetism and raw sex appeal. *Autumn* storm water makes one irresistible and bestows a Rasputin-like quality. This is the darkest and most dangerous of the lightning waters. Use with care and karmic consideration.

Lilac

RULER: Venus
TYPE: flower
MAGICKAL FORM: fresh, oil

This is the flirt flower. It attracts love quickly although the love doesn't last for long. Wear the oil or bathe in fresh lilacs when you want a fling. This flower is for fun. A great scent to spray in a room before parties or before meeting a date who is taking the relationship too seriously. Lilac keeps things light.

Lily

RULER: Moon
TYPE: flower
MAGICKAL FORM: fresh, oil

Place three lilies on the altar on the new moon to clear the way for new endeavors. The lily is very spiritual and considered a holy flower. It is sacred to the goddess in her maiden form and worked with to cleanse the soul and bring renewal. Wear the oil to conquer shyness or self-pity.

Lime

RULER: Sun
TYPE: fruit
MAGICKAL FORM: fruit, peel, oil

Suck on a lime if you want to release inhibitions. Lime is an aggressive ingredient and can be fickle and unpredictable when used in love formulas. It can, however, always be counted on to induce jealousy in another. This is the best ingredient for head games in relationships. It is an oil of power and added to commanding or compelling recipes to control situations. Carry the dried peel for protection and to keep evil schemes from overturning your plans.

Linden

RULER: Jupiter
TYPE: plant
MAGICKAL FORM: flower, tea

Drink linden tea for health and longevity. It is believed to be the flower of immortality. Add it to love ouangas or sprinkle in a circle around two red figure candles to make a love last forever.

Linen

RULER: Jupiter
TYPE: fabric
MAGICKAL FORM: white, purple

Spun from flax, linen holds a very spiritual vibration and makes dreams come true. Sleep on linen sheets to excel at astral travel. Use a pouch or ouanga made of linen for stuffing with psychic herbs. The fabric will multiply the power of the herbs and vastly increase your divinatory powers. Keep next to tarot cards or any tools of divination and hold against the third eye before doing any psychic work.

Lingam

RULER: Mars
TYPE: phallic image
MAGICKAL FORM: candle, statuary

Burn the lingam candle to attract a man or to increase male sexual stamina. Or burn one for healing male sexual diseases. Lingam statues on the altar draw down the creative energy of the god Mars.

Lobelia

RULER: Saturn
TYPE: plant
MAGICKAL FORM: powdered leaves, bark, flower

Medieval herbalists attribute many healing properties to this plant, however it is poisonous and should not be ingested or handled with bare hands. Add any form of lobelia to love formulas to prevent someone from leaving you. This borders on baneful magick, as it is working to control the will of another.

Lodestone

RULER: Saturn
TYPE: metal
MAGICKAL FORM: magnetically charged

The most powerful lodestones are the "hairy" ones. These magnetically charged stones are so thick with iron shavings that it almost appears as if hair is growing on the rock. Those with a smooth surface are weak and will not attract the energy you desire. Two lodestones placed in an ouanga along with appropriate herbs and oils will attract a long-term lover. Before placing them in the bag, make sure the lodestones cling to one another and do not repel each other. Add a single lodestone to a money or success ouanga (along with appropriate herbs and oils) to increase the drawing potential of the bag.

Lotus

RULER: Buddha, Saraswati
TYPE: plant
MAGICKAL FORM: oil, root

This is a holy plant used only for the highest of spiritual purposes. Place the roots around Buddha statues to bring enlightenment or around an image of the Hindu goddess Saraswati to elevate the mind. Lotus appeases the gods and should be offered when you feel you may have offended them and fallen out of their good graces. Wear the oil to tone down carnal urges. Anoint white candles with lotus oil and burn them for the deceased to elevate their souls.

Lovage

RULER: Pan, Astarte
TYPE: herb
MAGICKAL FORM: dried root

One of the most nonjudgmental of herbs, lovage draws the person most suited to your soul. A great root for bisexuals or anyone confused about which gender he or she is (or should be) attracted to. It is best used when invoking a new relationship and promises to quickly attract your heart's desire.

Lucky Hand

RULER: Fortuna, Jupiter
TYPE: root
MAGICKAL FORM: five fingered, fisted

These roots resemble the human hand. Do not use a broken one for ritual. The *five-fingered* or *open-handed* roots bring very good luck when carried in the pocket. Rub them with luck oils and place in a red ouanga bag for gambler's luck. Carry the *closed-fists* roots for protection from enemies.

M

Mace

RULER: Mercury
TYPE: herb
MAGICKAL FORM: powdered

The outer skin of the nutmeg is called mace and is completely different from the protective spray. Sprinkle some outside doors and windows for protection. Mace also stimulates brain activity and creativity. Smell the spice for inspiration, or mix with success formulas and burn as incense, or dust the hands with the powder.

Magnet

RULER: gods and goddesses of attraction
TYPE: metal
MAGICKAL FORM: horseshoe shape

The U-shaped, or horseshoe, magnet is used in all forms of manifestation magick. Work a simple spell by writing or painting the name of the petitioner across the bow of the magnet. Write requests, prayers, or petitions for love, health, success, or money on pieces of paper and then hold in place on an altar using the magnet. The altar must be of metal. Even a refrigerator door can serve as an altar. Place pictures or images of desires on the altar and hold in place by the magnet. The petitioner must place the right hand or right pointer finger through the loop of the magnet seven times daily for seven days and visualize themselves attracting the desired request into their lives. Do not remove the magnet and images fastened to the altar until the petition or desire is manifest.

Magnolia

RULER: Venus, Yemaya
TYPE: flower
MAGICKAL FORM: oil, flowers

There is no better flower for marriage or to influence a person to become more marriage-minded. Scratch your name and the name of the one you wish to marry onto a white candle and rub the candle with magnolia oil. Light it on a Friday on, or directly after, the new moon. Place the fresh or dried flowers underneath a bed where both parties sleep to bring about a marriage. Ground the dried flowers to a fine powder and sprinkle across a path where a reluctant partner is sure to walk.

Maidenhair

RULER: Venus
TYPE: fern plant
MAGICKAL FORM: leaves

Add some leaves to love spells to protect virginity. Maidenhair creates emotional bonds before sexual ones. Brew a tea with the leaves and add to the bathwater to enhance your beauty.

Makeup

RULER: Venus
TYPE: cosmetics
MAGICKAL FORM: blush, eyeliner, lipstick

During the Inquisition of the Middle Ages, many women were burned at the stake for no other reason than for wearing makeup or tinting the lips or hair. Makeup was considered a sign and tool of the witch or devil. Clearly, beauty products held a lot of power in those days. In ancient times, women such as Cleopatra infused her beauty products with the powers of seduction to win her men. All makeup can be applied with visualization to attract love or conquest. To do this, simply place the items in your hands and hold them over your heart. Say: "I dedicate these tools of beauty to Venus. I empower them with her beauty, and power of seduction. May they serve me well in conquest and in love. So mote it be." Continue to hold the items for two more minutes in both hands while visualizing the type of impression you want to make. Then begin to apply your makeup.

Malachite

RULER: Venus
TYPE: mineral
MAGICKAL FORM: raw or polished gemstone, egg shaped

This stone opens the subconscious and allows the wearer to understand his or her inner workings. It creates balance and fosters emotional nurturing and transformation. Malachite always picks up the wearer's feelings. It is a great stone to give to a secret crush or anyone to whom you want to transfer your love. Use it as a healing tool to cleanse the kidneys and liver of toxins. Malachite is a stone of wisdom and leadership. Wear it to stand out in a crowd.

Mandarin

RULER: Buddha, Mercury
TYPE: fruit
MAGICKAL FORM: flesh

Keep a bowl of mandarin oranges in the kitchen to bring cheerfulness and relaxation. Eat some to calm the nerves. Serve mandarins at gatherings to draw people out of their shells. This fruit attracts fun, laughter, and friendship.

Mandrake

RULER: Mercury and Hecate
TYPE: plant
MAGICKAL FORM: root

Known as the sorcerers' root, the mandrake is widely used in many forms of magick. Soak the root in water or brew like a tea then sprinkle this water around the home to protect from all evil and bad witchcraft. Do not drink this water or eat this root because the mandrake is *poisonous*. Carry the root in the pocket along with silver coins to increase wealth. Use whole roots to create powerful love poppets. Choose two whole roots that resemble the human form. Bind them together with red string or cord to create a long-lasting relationship between you and your mate.

Mango

RULER: Venus, Yemaya
TYPE: fruit
MAGICKAL FORM: whole, skin, pulp, juice

Mango is a popular love tonic. Drink the pulp or juice of the mango to increase sexual attraction, stimulation, and stamina. Requests for love can also be carved on the surface of the mango and then offered to Yemaya, the goddess of the sea, as a petition for romantic fulfillment. Use the skin of the mango in protection rites. Pull the skin from the mango until a large portion of the inner skin is exposed. Carve the name of an enemy, or someone who is trying to harm you, on the inside of the skin. Pull the rest of the skin from the fruit. Roll the skin up and bury it in earth or a pot of soil. In this way, you separate your enemy from yourself and remove any harm intended toward you or influence he or she may have upon you.

Maple

RULER: Jupiter
TYPE: tree
MAGICKAL FORM: leaf, syrup

One of the blessed trees, the maple brings sweetness to life and attracts wealth and wisdom. Place leaves on a prosperity altar or under your pillow to sweeten dreams and make them prophetic. Add the syrup to grains, cereals, bread products such as waffles or pancakes to "sweeten the pot." This is a great formula for gambler's luck and also to ensure that your good fortune brings you happiness. When good news is delivered, a dab of maple syrup held under the tongue ensures that the situation will be long lasting.

Marigold

RULER: Sun
TYPE: flower
MAGICKAL FORM: fresh or dried flowers, seeds, tea

Also called calendula, the marigold has healing properties and is used as a natural antifungal, antiseptic, and antibacterial treatment. Add the fresh flowers to salad greens and eat to promote good health and strengthen the immune system. Make a tea by steeping the flowers and drink to solve love problems. Pour a quart of the tea into your bathwater on a Sunday to increase your popularity and admiration among peers. The seeds are sacred to Apollo and, when eaten, bring visions.

Marjoram

RULER: Mercury
TYPE: spice
MAGICKAL FORM: ground or whole leaves

When placed inside a coffin with the deceased or grown on top of a grave, this herb is said to deliver the soul safely into the next world. When carried by living persons, it cures depression. Add marjoram to food to promote love and happiness between family members. It is a great herb to burn before saying "I love you" to a partner for the first time because it guarantees that these words will be mirrored back.

Marshmallow

RULER: Mercury, Apollo
TYPE: herb, confection
MAGICKAL FORM: root

Also known as Althea, the root of the marshmallow plant is used in healing and communication rituals. Grind the root to a powder and sprinkle on health or creativity altars on Wednesdays or Sundays to draw positive vibrations. Eat *marshmallow*, the confection, for love and comfort. Have some with sweet potatoes or yams, to increase fertility. Or eat it with chocolate to glean more pleasure and emotional satisfaction.

Marzipan

RULER: Mercury, Venus
TYPE: food
MAGICKAL FORM: flower and fruit shaped

This paste made of almonds and sugar is a perfect offering for the gods and goddesses of love and success. Shaped into the form of a flower, it makes an ideal love offering. Make a request for love as you place it on the altar or under a tree on a Friday on (or a few days before) the full moon. Give fruit-shaped candies in exchange for success and prosperity. Make your request as you leave these offerings on the altar or under an open sky on a Wednesday. Always make a wish before eating marzipan to make your wish come true.

Mastic

RULER: Mercury, Asclepios
TYPE: tree
MAGICKAL FORM: gum resin, oil

The small pea-shaped tears of this highly prized resin summon the creative powers of Mercury. Burn mastic as a devotional to the god of communication or rub the oil into orange candles to bring inspiration. Chew small pieces of it to improve communication and writing skills. It's a great cure for writer's block. The gum resin also has medicinal properties and can be offered with prayer to the god Asclepios to heal by magick.

Mayonnaise

RULER: Moon
TYPE: condiment
MAGICKAL FORM: white, yellow

Originally a very exclusive sauce from Spain and France, mayonnaise has evolved into an everyday American condiment. It now symbolizes bringing the extravagant to the mundane or wealth to the poor. Spread on bread or mix with salads to ward off poverty and fear of failure. The main ingredients are soybean (or vegetable) oil, eggs, vinegar, salt, sugar, and lemon juice. Soybean is an oil of prosperity and draws employment. Eggs, lemon, and vinegar remove negativity and any obstacles to well-being. Salt and sugar attract prosperity.

Meadowsweet

RULER: Sun
TYPE: herb
MAGICKAL FORM: dried leaves

Add this herb to incense or powders for healing, happiness, peace, and protection. Bathe in meadowsweet to reveal solutions to love problems.

Melissa

RULER: Sun
TYPE: herb
MAGICKAL FORM: dried leaves, oil

Drink the tea to calm fears. Mix with chamomile tea to alleviate stress and cure depression. The scent of melissa is uplifting. Place drops in a bowl of water or mist a room to lift the mood of those within. Bathing in the herb is believed to regulate the menstrual cycle.

Mercury

RULER: Mercury
TYPE: chemical
MAGICKAL FORM: liquid, beads

In Spanish spiritual rituals, beads of liquid mercury were scattered across the floor in order to divine the future. Because mercury is highly toxic, this ritual is extremely dangerous and should not be attempted. Liquid mercury is also a popular ingredient in gambling spells, and here liquid mastic or the beads of the mastic resin can be used as a safer substitute. Here is a spell for gambler's luck. Drill a small hole in the top of a buckeye and fill it with liquid mastic oil or the resinous beads. Then seal the hole with the wax drippings of a green candle. Hold this talisman in both hands while chanting: "Bring me luck. Quicksilver and Buck. Wax of green improve my luck. Bring me fortune by Quicksilver and Buck." Then place the buckeye in a green cloth bag and carry it in your pocket when gambling or picking lottery numbers.

Mesquite

RULER: Mars, Aztec sun god
TYPE: wood
MAGICKAL FORM: incense, smoked wood

Burn this wood for purification and healing. Mesquite energizes the spirits. Meats smoked in mesquite will fuel and energize instead of making those who eat it feel heavy or weighed down. Burn mesquite incense when you feel tired and need rejuvenation.

Milk

RULER: Moon, Hathor, Venus, Mercury, Ellegua
TYPE: dairy product
MAGICKAL FORM: whole

Cow's milk is one of the best magickal ingredients for spells to summon nurturing, prosperity, and protection. *Goat's milk* brings power and success. Use *soy milk* for job success and *coconut milk* for protection and spiritual cleansing. You can bathe in all types of milk for ritual purposes. The best time for milk baths is on Mondays or new or full moons.

Mimosa

RULER: Moon
TYPE: flower
MAGICKAL FORM: flower, oil

Place this "flower of dreams" under the pillow to remember your dreams, and also to make them come true. Pregnant women use the oil for protection and to ensure a safe gestation period. Rub a small amount into the belly for a healthy pregnancy. Place fresh flowers on a fertility altar when trying to conceive.

Mint

RULER: Mars, Pluto
TYPE: herb
MAGICKAL FORM: leaf, extract, oil

Legend holds that mint was originally the nymph Minte, lover of Pluto, the god of the underworld, who was turned into a mint plant by a jealous rival. *Peppermint* is called the lust herb. Chew on whole fresh leaves to increase sexual stamina. Chew *spearmint* leaves or rub the oil on the forehead or white candles to increase memory and intelligence. Add *wintergreen* oil or sprinkle the herb to baths and floor washes for protection.

Mirror

RULER: Hecate, Narcissus
TYPE: glass
MAGICKAL FORM: black or reflective

A blackened mirror is sacred to Hecate, the triple goddess of divination, and used for scrying or gazing to see the future or past. To create one, you must paint the reflective side of a mirror black. Gaze into the mirror until your eyes begin to tear; visions will then occur. Regular mirrors are sacred to Narcissus and relate to beauty magic. A mirror can be "witched" to create a more beautiful reflection. To accomplish this, wash the mirror down with apple cider vinegar and orange blossom water. Hexed mirrors contain evil spirits placed inside. To cleanse a mirror from evil, clean with ammonia and water.

Mistletoe

RULER: Apollo, Druids, Venus
TYPE: herb
MAGICKAL FORM: berries, leaves

Said to lose its power once it touches the ground, mistletoe is a holy herb and sacred to many deities. Kissing a lover under the mistletoe will make this relationship last. Adding mistletoe to other love potions increases their power. Place the leaves or berries high on a mantel in the home to protect its occupants. Leave a sprig of mistletoe in the home of someone you want to be remembered by. The leaves and berries of mistletoe are poisonous. Use caution when handling and keep away from small children and pets.

Mojo Beans

RULER: Jupiter, Chango
TYPE: bean
MAGICKAL FORM: beaded, loose

These hard red beans are also called African wishing beans. Wear them in a necklace or bracelet or carry loose beans in a red conjure or mojo bag for good luck. Make a wish on a mojo bean and carry for nine days. Then throw it in a river to make your wish come true.

Molasses

RULER: Scorpio, Mars, Pluto, Chango
TYPE: syrup
MAGICKAL FORM: darker the better

Use this syrup for controlling and compelling magic. Molasses is great to summon strength for hard work. Add three large tablespoonfuls to bathwater to create a stick-to-itiveness quality and increase your drive. Use in money magic along with honey and coins to draw business into an establishment. Offer cigars dipped or cured in molasses to Chango for business success. Scry in a bowl of molasses to gain wisdom and messages from Hecate, the dark mother.

Moldavite

RULER: extraterrestrials
TYPE: mineral
MAGICKAL FORM: chunks

This mineral was formed when a meteor hit the earth. Use the stone in meditation and ritual to communicate with aliens. It is a great channeling aid and creates spiritual mutation and evolution when added to the bathwater.

Monday

RULER: Moon
TYPE: day of the week
MAGICKAL FORM: sunrise and the eighth, sixteenth, and twenty-fourth hours of the day

A god, goddess, or planet governs each day of the week. It

is easy to spot the ruler of the day by its name. In the word *Monday*, we can see part of the word *Moon*. In the romance languages such as Italian or Spanish, this day of the week is called Lunes and clearly relates to the word *lunar*. On Mondays, a variety of magick may be worked. Check whether the moon is waning or waxing to determine what your spell will be. During waning moons, do spells to rid yourself of obstacles or for wisdom and protection. During waxing moons do magick for increase of any kind or to draw something into your life. Mondays are best for love magick and anything concerning home or family. The best hour to work is moonrise. Get this information from your local newspaper or a good astrological ephemeris.

Moonstone

RULER: Moon
TYPE: mineral
MAGICKAL FORM: pink or milky white gemstone

Supposedly infused with the light of the moon, this gemstone holds the power of prophecy and divination. It also lends great protection to its wearer. Use moonstones to tell the future and to increase psychic awareness. Wear the pink- or rose-colored stones near the heart to attract love.

Morning Glory

RULER: Sun, Apollo
TYPE: plant
MAGICKAL FORM: seeds

These seeds were eaten by the Aztecs to bring visions.

Their molecular structure resembles that of LSD. The seeds are sold in nurseries for planting. Using the seeds as a hallucinogenic is not only illegal but they are harmful when ingested. Grind to a fine powder and add to flying incense to gain psychic sight.

Moss

RULER: Jupiter
TYPE: plant
MAGICKAL FORM: green or brown

Add some to luck or money spells to keep a good financial situation growing strong.

Mouth

RULER: Mercury
TYPE: body part
MAGICKAL FORM: open or closed

One of the most magickal body parts, the mouth chants rituals and reveals the word of God and Goddess in pagan rites. The drawing down of God or Goddess is a sacred rite in which the priestess or priest is possessed by the deity and allows the deity to speak with his or her lips. The mouth or lips are also used to perform the kiss, one of the sacred signs of Wiccan rituals. A closed mouth can contain or hold energy. An open mouth reveals the word.

Muguet

RULER: Venus
TYPE: flower
MAGICKAL FORM: fresh or dried flowers, oil

A famous French courting oil, this fragrance attracts romantic encounters. Place the fresh flowers on an altar to attract a new love. Bathe in fresh or dried flowers to bring more romance into a relationship. Rub the oil onto a pink candle to woo or be wooed.

Mugwort

RULER: Moon
TYPE: herb
MAGICKAL FORM: fresh sprig, dried herb, tea

Drink mugwort tea on a dark moon to reveal Armageddon-type prophecies. Drink on a new moon to gain spiritual possibilities of a more positive nature. Drink mugwort tea on a full moon to fulfill desires in love. Wash crystal balls in a warm mugwort bath to increase their clarity. Add mugwort to any love potion to gain access to feelings of another and to bond psychically with a lover. Carry a fresh sprig to bring safety in travel and prevent obstacles and delays on the road.

Mulberry

RULER: Mercury
TYPE: tree
MAGICKAL FORM: wood, berries

Add the berries to success spells for insight and inspiration. A mulberry wand will bring more focus and clarity to ritual. It helps to center the practitioner, increase magickal awareness, and bring sudden insight or revelation.

Mullein

RULER: Saturn
TYPE: plant
MAGICKAL FORM: powdered leaves

Burn this herb of exorcism to chase demons from the house. Referred to as graveyard dust (or used as a substitute for the real thing), mullein is used in hexing spells and is often sprinkled over the picture of an enemy to bring him bad luck. Mullein is most effective when used by men in love spells to drive away competition and keep their woman faithful.

Mushroom

RULER: Neptune
TYPE: vegetable
MAGICKAL FORM: raw, cooked

This is the flower of illusion and many mushrooms are actually hallucinogenic. All mushrooms hold the property of fantasy and are eaten to invoke glamour or to create illusions.

For love they should be cooked in soups with paprika and/or fish. To create glamours, or illusions, eat them raw. Native Americans use the magic mushroom in rites to produce visions or embark on vision quests.

Musk

RULER: Venus, Adonis
TYPE: fragrance
MAGICKAL FORM: crystals, oil

A prized ingredient of perfumes for centuries, the true musk oil will be difficult to obtain. Since it is derived from the intestinal sac of the male musk deer, it is illegal in many countries. Use a chemical compound (such as synthesized muscone) in place of the original scent. Musk is worn to alleviate loneliness and to attract love. Mixed with more fiery ingredients, such as red sandalwood and cinnamon, it promotes lust. The crystals can be burned or added to bathwater to create greater sensuality. Rub the oil into the skin to increase awareness of potential mates or to strengthen the emotional bonds of an already existing relationship. Wear musk to increase popularity and allure.

Mustard

RULER: Mars
TYPE: spice
MAGICKAL FORM: seed, spread

Known as the great awakener, mustard opens the brain centers to increase alertness and awareness. It is a great condiment to add to the diet to enhance the memory. Eat while studying for exams to help your memory. Mustard also gives strength and courage when facing difficulty. The seed can be sprinkled in the shoe or across a path to promote desire.

Myrrh

RULER: Saturn, Isis
TYPE: resin, plant
MAGICKAL FORM: resinous beads, powder, oil

One of the holiest scents of the Bible and one of the gifts of the Magi to the baby Jesus, myrrh is the feminine complement to frankincense. Burned together, they can balance out the yin and yang. Myrrh is both bitter and sweet. Use the bitter fragrance to deal with sorrow. Burn it to gain wisdom when you are mourning the loss of someone or something. Add the sweet variety to love spells to deepen their effects.

Myrtle

RULER: Venus
TYPE: plant
MAGICKAL FORM: leaves, oil

Use this precious fragrance sparingly. A single drop in a love potion will cause significant infatuation. The myrtle also brings gentleness and can calm the spirit. It is a plant of peace and humanitarian love as well as sexual love. Leaves placed on an altar to Venus attract her devotion. Use when you need more commitment from a partner.

Nails, Finger- and Toe-

RULER: cemetery deities
TYPE: body part
MAGICKAL FORM: clippings

Much superstition surrounds the cutting of fingernails and toenails. It is believed that the soul can be captured through them. In many cultures, the nail clippings are saved throughout one's life and buried with the person. The belief is that the soul cannot enter heaven without all the body parts intact. It's not surprising then that you can use nail clippings in sympathetic magic to control another's actions. Fingernail clippings from the right hand influence actions, from the left hand influence the heart, and toenail clippings will lead someone to walk a certain path.

Nails, Iron

RULER: Saturn
TYPE: metal
MAGICKAL FORM: rusty, iron

An iron nail found near a railroad track brings good luck. Carry a bent nail for protection. Collect rusty nails and add them to witches' bottles of protection to keep evil energy away from the home and its occupants. Use caution when collecting and handling rusty nails.

Naked

RULER: God, Goddess
TYPE: form of practice
MAGICKAL FORM: the body

Going skyclad, or naked, in Wiccan rites is a sign that you are truly free. Some covens are robed, some are naked underneath the robes, and some are completely skyclad (depending on the weather). Nudity is the great equalizer, and in Wicca the human form is celebrated and liberated during sacred rites.

Names

RULER: gods, goddesses
TYPE: magickal custom
MAGICKAL FORM: personal

Traditionally in Wicca the priest or priestess chooses a new name upon initiation. This name is used in all magic circles and ritual. In fact, some covens impose punishment on those who forget and use common names within the magic circle. Magickal names are usually meaningful to the individual, and men and women often choose the names of gods or goddesses who have qualities they desire. Some witches choose names of herbs or stars or planets. A magickal name is very personal; its purpose is to lift the practitioner out of the mundane and to open up the spiritual or magickal side of the personality while in the "other" world. When witches were persecuted, the names were used to protect their identities.

Narcissus

RULER: Dionysus
TYPE: plant
MAGICKAL FORM: flower, oil

Wear this scent to entice others and promote self-love and self-confidence. Overuse can attract stalkers and create egomaniacs. Rub on pink candles to meet new people. Rub *black narcissus* oil on black candles for self-hypnosis. Use the oil on red candles to hypnotize and bewitch another.

Neptune

RULER: ocean
TYPE: god, planet
MAGICKAL FORM: shells, coral, color blue, seaweed, anything from the ocean

This god of the ocean can be summoned in spells to reveal treasures from the deep. Use his energy to gain riches and unconditional love. As a planetary energy, Neptune rules illusions and psychic powers.

Neroli

RULER: Jupiter
TYPE: flower
MAGICKAL FORM: flower, oil

This is one of the best scents to use in marriage spells. Wear it when you want to attract a marriage-minded mate or rub onto pink candles to get a proposal from the one you love. Neroli is found in bridal bouquets to bless the union of a couple with prosperity. Rub it into yellow or gold candles and light for fame and personal recognition.

Nettle

RULER: Saturn
TYPE: plant
MAGICKAL FORM: tea, dried leaves

Drink nettle tea for purification. To remove a jinx, add the tea to floor wash or bathwater. Scatter the loose leaves outside a home to remove negativity.

Newsprint

RULER: Mercury
TYPE: paper
MAGICKAL FORM: pulverized

Shred the front page of a newspaper and put it in a blender to pulverize. Then add the powder to success formulas or incense when you want media coverage.

Nightshade

RULER: Hecate
TYPE: plant
MAGICKAL FORM: roots, leaves, tops

Also called belladona or deadly nightshade, this plant is poisonous and should never be ingested. Add it to flying ointment or incense to gain psychic powers. It can also be added to witches' bottles of protection.

Nosegay

RULER: Venus
TYPE: flowers
MAGICKAL FORM: hand-picked flower bouquet

Giving flowers is a very powerful form of love magick. Historically, it is part of the etiquette of courtship, but when given with magickal intent, this ritual can have added meaning and effect. Bouquets must be handpicked to maximize their magickal effects. *White* flowers open the way to pure love. *Pink* flowers are flirtatious, and *red* flowers open sexual channels. A mixture of all three colors promotes a healthy, fully rounded relationship. Use *purple* flowers to win someone back. *Yellow* is the color of admiration but also denotes jealousy, so be careful with its use. Don't deliver a nosegay by messenger; you must deliver it by hand to the one you wish to magickally influence. Your eyes must then lock as the flowers pass from hand to hand for the magick to take full effect.

Numbers

RULER: various gods and goddesses
TYPE: measure of counting
MAGICKAL FORM: 1 to 10 archetypal

Many deities are associated with numbers and magick always works better when the user is aware of them and uses specific numbers in their spells. This may determine the number of lit candles or offerings given, or it may suggest that a certain hour of the day will favor the spell. Here are the numbers for the most common deities and planets invoked in ritual.

> *Jupiter—4*
> *Venus—7*
> *Moon—3*
> *Mars—5*
> *Mercury—8*
> *Sun—6*
> *Ellegua—3*
> *Oshun—5 and all multiples of 5*
> *Hecate—3*

Nutmeg

RULER: Jupiter
TYPE: spice
MAGICKAL FORM: whole, powdered, oil

A gambler's favorite, nutmeg is used for luck; it promotes winning in games of chance. Nutmeg is also a psychic inducer so it helps to pick winning lottery numbers. Hold the whole nutmeg in your hand when gambling to increase your luck. Dust the hands with the powder or add to success formulas when you need to use your intuition to succeed. Rub the oil into purple candles for power and roll green candles in nutmeg powder to invoke a spirit of generosity.

Nuts

RULER: Jupiter, Mercury
TYPE: food
MAGICKAL FORM: whole, crushed

All nuts promote communication; they are great to put out at parties or mixers to get people talking. The nut is a food of

laughter and joy. They can be used in money, luck, and love spells. Nuts also bring quick results. Use *almonds* for love; hold under the tongue to intuit a lover's needs. Eat *walnuts* to increase earnings and to get a raise or find employment. *Peanuts* prevent poverty. Eat *pine nuts* for lust and *hazelnuts* for wisdom. *Pistachio* is a love nut, especially the red ones. Use *white (natural) pistachios* as fertility charms. Eat *pecans* for financial security, *chestnuts* for love and wisdom, and *cashews* for luck and long-lasting love. *Brazil nuts* open channels and increase luck. *Double nuts* are the luckiest of all; make a wish while chewing one.

O

Oak

RULER: Sun
TYPE: tree
MAGICKAL FORM: acorn, bark, trees

Sacred to the Druids, the oak branch makes an ideal witches' wand. Standing under the tree grants protection, strength, and longevity. Acorns were used to ward off lightning and can be carried for fertility and prosperity. Add the bark to incense for strength and grounding.

Oak Moss

RULER: Jupiter
TYPE: plant
MAGICKAL FORM: moss, oil

Add the dried moss to money and luck formulas. Rub the dark musky oil on your feet for grounding and sensuality.

Oat

RULER: Venus
TYPE: grain
MAGICKAL FORM: raw, cooked

A grain of prosperity, raw oats are sprinkled in harvest rituals in the fall to honor the Earth Mother and thank her for her gifts of bounty. Eat bread with oats to increase your income. Cook and eat *oatmeal* (not instant) when you are looking for employment.

Oath

RULER: god and goddess of the witches
TYPE: spoken word
MAGICKAL FORM: blood oath

Witches take oaths during initiation and swear to protect the secrets of the craft. The oath is accompanied by drawing blood from the initiate. This blood is then soaked into red cord and kept by the priest or priestess. Should the initiate break his or her oath, the cord will be used in magick to harm the oath breaker. In many covens, the cord is returned to the initiate in good faith. When witches were burned at the stake, the sworn oath was necessary to prevent initiates from harming other witches by revealing their names. Unfortunately, in the modern world, the oath is often used incorrectly to intimidate and hold power over new initiates.

Obsidian

RULER: Saturn
TYPE: mineral
MAGICKAL FORM: raw or cut and polished stone

Carry this stone or meditate upon it to break through illusions and to reveal deceptions. Obsidian brings balance and grounding and promotes realistic thinking.

Oil

RULER: water
TYPE: liquid
MAGICKAL FORM: fragrance, essential

Any herb or flower prepared in the form of oil will have strong emotional effects on the user. Rub the oils into pulse points on the body. Use it to scent candles and rooms to create magickal effects. Essential oils are best but sometimes difficult to obtain. An oil can be used on its own or combined with other oils to layer magickal results.

Ointments

RULER: earth, water
TYPE: solid mixture
MAGICKAL FORM: prepared on dark, new, or full moon phases

Ointments are considered more powerful than oils or loose herbs. Prepare the ointment by slow boiling or double boiling a mixture of herbs and essential oils in a base of coconut or olive oil. Then rub the ointment into the skin so it is quickly absorbed into the bloodstream. Popular ointments are those for love or flying. The flying ointment is prepared with hallucinogenic ingredients and rubbed into the skin to "gain the sight" or induce psychic visions.

Oleander

RULER: Pluto, Osiris
TYPE: plant
MAGICKAL FORM: flower, oil

The presence of this flower is said to appease the spirits of the dead. Place on a gravesite as a prayer for a loved one to gain eternal peace. Rub the flower's oil into white candles to persuade ghosts or spirits to depart. It is the best remedy to sweeten negative spirits and compel them to move on. Handle with care, as oleander is a poisonous shrub. Wear gloves when working with flower or essential oil.

Olibanum

RULER: Sun
TYPE: plant
MAGICKAL FORM: beads or pearls, oil

Used in biblical times, this holy scent is very similar to (and can be substituted for) frankincense. Burn to purify a room and call good spirits to your aid. Wear the scent when preparing for a spiritual journey.

Olive

RULER: Sun, Athena
TYPE: plant
MAGICKAL FORM: branch, oil, fruit

This sacred tree was honored by many ancient civilizations and is said to be a gift from the goddess Athena. The olive represents wisdom, longevity, protection, and prosperity. The branch of the tree symbolizes peace and can be given or kept to heal anger. The oil makes a great base for ointments or oil blends and adds success and prosperity to the blend. Cook with olive oil or eat olives to invoke long life. Consume *green olives* for wealth. *Black olives* bring protection and *red olives* love.

Onion

RULER: Mars
TYPE: vegetable
MAGICKAL FORM: red, white, yellow, purple

Use this many-layered food to peel away problems in life and to dispel anger. The onion is also a love food and is said to increase male virility. *Red onions* promote lust when added to dishes. *White onions* clear away obstacles when peeled to the core. Use *purple onions* for power and seduction. *Yellow onions* dispel anger between friends. Carve the names of quarreling parties into a yellow onion and keep until it forms roots. At this time, the two friends or family members will begin to recall the positive roots of their relationship and let go of their anger toward each other. Do not get rid of the onion until apologies have been made and accepted. You may then offer the onion to the earth in thanks.

Onyx

RULER: Mars
TYPE: mineral
MAGICKAL FORM: polished or unpolished gems

Wear or meditate upon this stone for strength, courage, stamina, focus, and determination in accomplishing tasks. It brings self-control and achievement. Prolonged use or wearing of onyx results in happiness and fulfillment of dormant potential.

Opal

RULER: Venus
TYPE: mineral
MAGICKAL FORM: polished

This is the trickster stone. It is hard to hold on to and many are superstitious about wearing it because it brings all the emotions to the surface. Those born under the sign of

Libra will have the most success with this gemstone. Wear or meditate upon it to draw love and faithful companions. Rub the stone to create more spontaneity in life.

Opium

RULER: Venus
TYPE: perfume scent
MAGICKAL FORM: oil

Wear this oil for the power of seduction. Add to love incense to create more lust and passion. Anoint the third eye to dream prophetically.

Orange

RULER: Buddha, Venus, Juno
TYPE: fruit
MAGICKAL FORM: fresh, dried peel, oil

In China, the orange is a symbol of gold and prosperity. Leave as an offering next to a Buddha statue to increase your luck and wealth. The Greek god Jove gave Juno an orange blossom on their wedding day. Both the fruit and the flower are a symbol of committed love. Surround white and red candles with dried orange peel or rub orange oil into them for a love and commitment spell. *Blood oranges* excite the passions when eaten. The *color orange* symbolizes success, energy, spiritual evolvement, and creativity.

Orchid

RULER: Venus
TYPE: flower
MAGICKAL FORM: fresh
flower, oil

A symbol of power, uniqueness, and charisma, orchid oil or flowers are added to love and success spells to increase your sexual allure. Orchids are best in love spells when you need a competitive edge. Bathe in the petals to get noticed.

Oregano

RULER: Jupiter
TYPE: spice
MAGICKAL FORM: dried

A common household spice, oregano adds flavor to foods but also enhances magickal flavor to spells. Add some to money, health, or love recipe to increase your pleasure and satisfaction with the results.

Orris

RULER: Venus
TYPE: plant
MAGICKAL FORM: root, powder, oil

Dust your body with the powder to attract a lover. It also

promotes playfulness and increases sexual pleasure. Carry the root to make a relationship last longer. Rub orris oil into red candles to release inhibitions. It's a great "coming-out" oil for gays and lesbians.

Owl

RULER: Hecate
TYPE: bird
MAGICKAL FORM: live, image

Many believe that the hooting of an owl or the spying of one is a portent of the arrival of death. Witches believe that seeing an owl precedes a divine message or prophecy about the future. This message will often be of a serious nature and is usually given to offset danger. Owl candles, bells, and statues are placed on the witches' altar to symbolize the power of Hecate. They represent her wisdom.

Oysters

RULER: Neptune, Venus
TYPE: shellfish
MAGICKAL FORM: raw

One of the most powerful aphrodisiacs, oysters represent the female genitalia and are eaten by women to increase orgasmic pleasure. Men eat them to make themselves more intuitive and better lovers. Oysters are also eaten for fertility.

Paella

RULER: Venus
TYPE: prepared dish
MAGICKAL FORM: cooked with visualization

Feasting is part of Wiccan magick. Sometimes when the circle or ritual is concluded, coven members share a meal. Paella is a Spanish dish and one of the favorites to prepare for summer rituals. Traditionally it is made with yellow rice, vegetables, sausage, chicken, and seafood. As the paella is prepared and eaten, prosperity is visualized. The meat, chicken, and vegetables bring blessings of the earth. The seafood brings the bounty of the sea, and the yellow rice happiness, good fortune, and long life.

Palm

RULER: Jove
TYPE: plant
MAGICKAL FORM: leaves

Autumn rituals for blessing and purification, and winter rituals for protection, use palm leaves, or fronds. Wave the palm frond in all four directions and then above and below. Fronds are also used to make a cross to bless your oil with magick. Cut a slit in one leaf and place another leaf through the slit so that one leaf is horizontal and the other vertical, forming the shape of the cross. Place the cross in a bottle of olive oil and use the now holy oil for spiritual work or serious protection. Rub the oil into your skin or onto white candles. Or burn the palm leaf cross and rub the ashes on your forehead for purification or add them to spiritual cleansing incenses.

Palmarosa

RULER: Venus
TYPE: plant
MAGICKAL FORM: oil, tincture

A refreshing and calming fragrance, palmarosa can be sprayed around a room to reduce stress. It is also used in skin treatments and beauty spells to restore youthfulness.

Pancakes

RULER: Mercury
TYPE: prepared food
MAGICKAL FORM: round, buckwheat, with syrup

The flapjack, or pancake, dates from ancient Egypt and is a food of prosperity. Its three main ingredients—flour, milk, and eggs—symbolize life, nurturing, and rebirth. They are best eaten on the full moon or on a Tuesday to round out your fortune. Smother with syrup to attract more money. Also, eat pancakes to win races or athletic games.

Pansy

RULER: Mercury
TYPE: flower
MAGICKAL FORM: flowers

Use this flower to send astral messages of love. Place on top of a picture of one who is far away to get him or her to think of you. Add violet flowers to get someone to return a message to you.

Papaya

RULER: Venus
TYPE: fruit
MAGICKAL FORM: seeds, flesh, skin

This fruit is consumed for sex, fertility, and wealth. Eat fresh papaya to induce lust. Sprinkle the seeds over a river to conceive a child. Dry the skin and carry a small piece in the wallet as a money-drawing talisman.

Paprika

RULER: Venus
TYPE: spice
MAGICKAL FORM: sweet, hot

Season fish stews with this spice for prosperity. Add paprika to any meat dish or sprinkle on love altars for marriage rituals. The *sweet paprika* summons loyalty. The *spicy* blend invokes passion but overuse can result in jealousy.

Papyrus

RULER: Thoth
TYPE: plant
MAGICKAL FORM: paper

This is one of the holiest papers for drawing talismans. It is also common to have depictions of Egyptian gods or goddesses drawn on papyrus decorating the altar. Place prayers or requests written on papyrus into a bottle and drop it in a river in order for them to come true. Writers needing inspiration can charge their pens by wrapping them in papyrus scrolls while not in use.

Parchment

RULER: Mercury, Solomon
TYPE: paper made of animal skin
MAGICKAL FORM: squares

Made from sheepskin, parchment paper is easily found in art supply stores. Magicians prefer it to paper made from trees. The product made from animal skin is said to carry a stronger spiritual vibration and bring life to any seal or symbol drawn upon it. Draw parchment seals with magickal ink and carry them around for luck, love, money, or protection.

Parsley

RULER: ghosts and spirits of the underworld, Mercury
TYPE: herb
MAGICKAL FORM: fresh sprigs

The custom of placing a sprig of fresh parsley on a plate of cooked meat arose from the belief that the herb could appease the spirits of the dead animal. Parsley refreshes and renews and also rids an area of negative or fearful energy. Parsley placed in a room can tone down and alleviate poltergeist activity. Steep fresh sprigs in a bucket of warm water and mop the area, or place in a spray bottle and mist the room. Brush the dry sprigs across the Ouija board before working to calm the spirits and prevent any malevolent force from coming through. Parsley cleanses the body and soul of fear and renews the life force. Eat parsley to cleanse your feelings and get rid of any emotional baggage that is blocking you from experiencing loving relationships.

Parsnip

RULER: Mars
TYPE: vegetable
MAGICKAL FORM: root

Eat raw or add to soup for grounding and centering. Parsnip is good for saving money and getting out of debt. Snip the roots and add to mop water to prevent your home from draining you financially.

Passionflower

RULER: Moon
TYPE: herb
MAGICKAL FORM: dried

Burn or sprinkle for protection and well-being. The name of this flower is misleading; very rarely is it added to love spells as it actually cools the passions. This is one of the best herbs for dispelling anger and bad tempers. If someone is angry with you, sprinkle in a place where he is sure to walk across. To overcome your own anger, bathe in the herb or carry in a pouch on the left side of your body until you calm down.

Passion Fruit

RULER: Venus
TYPE: fruit
MAGICKAL FORM: seeds, flesh

Eat it to increase your fertility. Plant the seeds with wishes for the health of your children.

Pasta

RULER: Mercury
TYPE: food
MAGICKAL FORM: al dente or firm

Spiral pasta is the best choice for enhancing your creativity. Eat *spaghetti* or *linguine* for protection and to improve communication. *Corn* pasta helps bring financial creativity and *rice* pasta is good for love.

Patchouli

RULER: earth deities
TYPE: herb
MAGICKAL FORM: dried leaves, root, oil

This dark heady scent is easily obtained in essential oil form at pharmacies and in loose herbal form in occult shops. It is one of the most well-rounded and powerful plants for working a variety of spells. Its strongest property is that of grounding, but patchouli can be added to prosperity, love, sex, health, and protection formulas as well. It brings stability and comfort when worn by those in distress. It is also a natural antiseptic, so use it to ward off germs and get rid of negative vibes.

Pea

RULER: Venus
TYPE: vegetable
MAGICKAL FORM: pod, pea

Peace and prosperity are the magickal properties of the pea. Eat and serve the whole pod for family unity and well-being. Eat shucked peas on Fridays to alleviate money worries and solve love problems. Salt the peas to obtain answers to domestic concerns, whether emotional or financial. Eat raw peas for beauty.

Peach

RULER: Sun, Venus
TYPE: fruit
MAGICKAL FORM: flesh, pit

Dry and crush the pits to a fine powder and sprinkle over a red male or female figure candle to keep a partner from straying. Eat fresh peaches to bring happiness and long life.

Pear

RULER: Sun gods
TYPE: fruit, tree, essential oil

Eat pears in winter for health and on your birthday for longevity and wisdom. Rub the oil on red candles for stamina and endurance. The tree is a sacred site for blessings and the protection of children.

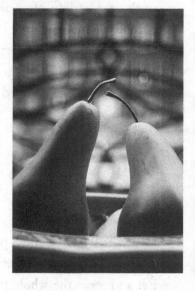

Pearl

RULER: Neptune, Venus
TYPE: mineral
MAGICKAL FORM: strands, loose

A stone of love and transformation, pearls open the heart and create positive emotional change when worn or carried. Add crushed pearls to potions to create illusions or glamours.

Pennies

RULER: Venus, Oshun
TYPE: coins
MAGICKAL FORM: heads up

Throw five pennies (heads up) into the bottom of a seven-day candle jar before inserting the candle. This brings added luck and power to your magick, especially if the candle is for love or money. Pick up a heads-up penny and carry for good luck. If a penny is heads down, don't take it, but turn it around and leave as a luck talisman for someone else to find.

Pennyroyal

RULER: Saturn
TYPE: herb
MAGICKAL FORM: dried leaves, oil

Wear the oil for protection and to repel annoying people. Brew the leaves into a tea for regulating the menstrual cycle. Do not use if you are pregnant, as this is one of the abortive herbs.

Pentagram

RULER: five elements
TYPE: geometric figure
MAGICKAL FORM: traced in air, carved on metal, drawn on paper or wax

Witches use the pentagram, or five-pointed star, for many magickal purposes. It is the witches' identifying emblem as much as the cross represents Christianity and the Star of

David is the symbol of Judaism. Witches wear a metal pentagram (traditionally made of silver or gold) for protection. Place copper pentacles upon the altar to bless and consecrate food and magickal tools. Trace the pentagram in the air to call down elemental quarters and also to dismiss them. Draw the *invoking pentagram* beginning at the top point of the star and pull the imaginary line down to the bottom left leg of the star. Move up on a diagonal to the right arm of the pentagram and then across to the left arm. Go down on a diagonal to the right leg and then back up to the top of the star. For the *banishing pentagram* begin at the lower left leg and draw an imaginary line away from yourself and up toward the top point of the star. Continue drawing down to the right leg of the pentagram, then move on the diagonal to the left arm, across to the right arm, and return to the left leg to complete the figure. Pentagrams are also drawn on parchment paper or cut into candles and burned for blessing and protection. The five points of the star represent earth, air, fire, water, and spirit. The upright pentagram represents the human form filled with divine energy. The inverted pentagram is a depiction of a person standing on his or her head. In other words, the genitals are placed above the brain, symbolizing the animal instincts of man as opposed to the rationality of man. For witches, the inverted pentagram symbolizes the second-degree initiation or journey through the underworld or abyss. It is the exploration of the darker side of one's nature. Some view the inverted pentagram as the horns of the devil and a tool of evil.

Peony

RULER: Sun
TYPE: plant
MAGICKAL FORM: root, flower

Place a peony under the pillow to chase away bad dreams and demons. Grow in a garden to protect the home. This is one of the best flowers to protect children.

Pepper, Spice

RULER: Mars
TYPE: spice
MAGICKAL FORM: ground, whole

Heat producing and fiery, chili pepper makes a great lust ingredient. Add to coconut and chocolate to turn up the flames of desire. Place a circle of *red peppercorns* around a photograph of your lover to keep others away from him or her. Pepper is also used for war and separation spells. Sprinkle *white pepper* in the corners of a room to overcome anger and dissention. *Black pepper* mixed with salt and sulfur gets rid of someone you don't want around.

Pepper, Vegetable

RULER: Jupiter, Venus
TYPE: vegetable
MAGICKAL FORM: green, red, purple, orange

If you are awaiting a money award in a court settlement, write the amount you want on a piece of paper. Cut a slit in a *green pepper* and place the piece of paper inside of it. Put the green pepper in the freezer and keep it there until you have won your case. Eat *red peppers* with a lover to improve your sex life, or *purple peppers* on Thursdays or full moons for power, protection, and wisdom. Eat orange peppers for creativity and spiritual evolvement.

Peppermint, *see* Mint

Perfume

RULER: Venus
TYPE: fragrance
MAGICKAL FORM: applied to pulse points

Anointing is one of the sacred rites of witches. Rubbing oils or perfumes into the pulse points gives the wearer greater power and influence than a random application or spray. Modern advertising campaigns promise users all sorts of magic by using specific perfumes and fragrances. To up the ante and make your scent more effective, anoint the wrists, inside elbows, behind the ears, under the armpits, the heart, inner thighs, behind the knees, and ankles.

Peridot

RULER: Venus
TYPE: mineral
MAGICKAL FORM: cut and polished

Wear or carry this stone to increase your psychic intuition. This gem of rejuvenation and relaxation is one of the best for stress reduction.

Periwinkle

RULER: Venus
TYPE: plant
MAGICKAL FORM: dried

Do not ingest this herb, as it is poisonous. Sprinkle under a bed to bump up your sex life. Periwinkle invokes fun and pleasure but it is also a plant of true love. Add to a dream pillow to be led to your soul mate.

Persimmon

RULER: Hermes, Aphrodite
TYPE: fruit
MAGICKAL FORM: flesh, seeds

This is the "strange" or "queer" fruit. Persimmons bring luck to gays, lesbians, transgender, and transsexual people. Eat the fruit to find your perfect lover. Carry the seeds in your pocket to be more successful with gender bending.

Pesto

RULER: Venus, Mars
TYPE: sauce
MAGICKAL FORM: fresh

This sauce is the perfect blend of love and money ingredients and always brings quick results. The pesto should be fresh, not store-bought. Prepare with walnuts to bring fast luck with money. Use pine nuts to fall in love.

Petitgrain

RULER: Venus
TYPE: plant
MAGICKAL FORM: fragrance, extract

Used in aromatherapy, petitgrain is derived from the bitter orange tree. Wear the scent to bring joy and lift the spirits. Rub into red candles to boast self-confidence. Rub into pink candles to calm the nerves.

Petrified Wood

RULER: Sun
TYPE: tree
MAGICKAL FORM: wand, altar ornamentation

A wand made of petrified wood or even a small piece kept on the altar will help you keep a good balance between the worlds. We've all met the "crazy witch" or the "new age nut" that seems to have gone totally over the deep end. Working with petrified wood will help you keep both feet on the ground and find a way to apply your spiritual insights to the everyday world. Hold on to a piece when you feel you are in danger of losing touch with reality.

Peyote

RULER: Neptune
TYPE: plant
MAGICKAL FORM: button

Native Americans used mescal for vision quests. Eat this hallucinogenic to alter consciousness and gain psychic sight.

Pickle

RULER: Mercury
TYPE: vegetable
MAGICKAL FORM: whole

Eat one on a Wednesday to open the imagination and create excitement. The pickle is a great remedy for boredom. Sliced or cut pickles do not hold any magickal power. They must be eaten whole for ritual use.

Picture

RULER: various
TYPE: paper
MAGICKAL FORM: photograph, image

In some cultures, it is still considered taboo to have your picture taken, as it is thought to capture your spirit and open you to possible manipulation. And it's true: you can definitely work magick through a photograph or someone else's belongings. Add pictures of loved ones (or enemies) to ouanga bags or surround their pictures with herbs to influence their lives. Use pictures of the infirm in meditation to send healing energy. It is considered bad luck to place a picture of a living person next to a burning candle. Place images of things you want to possess, such as a car or a home, on an altar so that they may become manifest.

Pie

RULER: Venus
TYPE: baked good
MAGICKAL FORM: various fillings

Originating in ancient Greece and Rome, pies are associated with happiness, love, and wholeness. Eat cherry pie to increase self-confidence and find self-love. All fruit pies invoke love when shared with another. Meat pies create feelings of security. Place your thumb in a pie and make a wish. (This is kind of rude unless you are eating alone.)

Pierogi

RULER: Moon
TYPE: dumpling
MAGICKAL FORM: various fillings

This Polish delicacy is best eaten on new and full moons. They are a comfort food and alleviate depression in the winter months. Eat *potato pierogis* for nurturing, *sweet potato pierogis* for love, *meat pierogis* for personal endurance, and *cabbage pierogis* for money. All pierogis are protective.

Pillow

RULER: Venus
TYPE: fabric stuffed with herbs and flowers
MAGICKAL FORM: hand sewn

Place sleep pillows stuffed with herbs by, or under, the head to influence the sleeper. Use white or blue cotton or silk cloth and thread. Chamomile and lavender are the best ingredients for a restful sleep. Add mimosa to dispel bad dreams and mugwort to make dreams prophetic. Love pillows should be stuffed with seven different ingredients (see Magickal Love Tables to help you choose your ingredients) into pink or red silk cloth and sewn with cotton thread. Hold the pillow to the heart while falling asleep to bring love into your life.

Pimiento

RULER: Mars
TYPE: vegetable
MAGICKAL FORM: fermented, pickled

These heart-shaped sweet peppers are usually found stuffed in small green olives. Eat pimientos to prolong a love relationship. They are best eaten on Fridays on or close to the full moon.

Pine

RULER: Sun
TYPE: tree
MAGICKAL FORM: branch, cone, needles, oil

Cleansing, health, and energy are the magickal properties of the pine. A pine wand or pinecone kept on the altar wards off evil influences. Floor washes with pine oil cleanse a space of negativity and ward off illness. Throw pine needles into winter fires for protection, or burn pine incense for purification and divination.

Pineapple

RULER: Sun
TYPE: fruit
MAGICKAL FORM: fruit, dried peel

Eat pineapple for prosperity. Consume this "family values" fruit to ensure fidelity and happy marriages. Dry the peel and pulverize to add to money formulas, especially when you are looking for income to buy something extravagant.

Pink

RULER: Venus
TYPE: color
MAGICKAL FORM: candles, cloth

This color is used in magick when dealing with flirtation and sexuality. It is the best color to work with when trying to attract a new love. Pink is also a calming and relaxing color and is used to reduce fears.

Pins

RULER: Saturn
TYPE: metal
MAGICKAL FORM: safety, straight

Most people can easily conjure up an image of a voodoo doll stuck with pins, and usually associate such activity with cursing or "black magick." But pins are actually used in dolls for healing, much like psychic acupuncture needles. They pinpoint and release pain. Pins are also lucky. Pick up a pin found in the street (carefully) and keep it in a jar for protection and good luck. Place open safety pins on altars or on a high kitchen shelf to prevent poverty.

Pizza

RULER: Sun
TYPE: food
MAGICKAL FORM: round, triangle

Whole pizzas should be blessed with prosperity before being consumed. Eat a triangular single slice when things seem very difficult and you feel you need a lucky break with any situation in your life. The Sicilian, or square, pizza does not hold any magickal properties.

Plantain

RULER: Earth
TYPE: plant
MAGICKAL FORM: cooked flesh or dried skin

Cook the *green plantain* and eat it to attract prosperity. Fry the *ripe, sweet plantain* and eat it to draw love. Dry the skin and wrap in red cord and hang above a doorway as a talisman of protection.

Plum

RULER: Uranus
TYPE: fruit
MAGICKAL FORM: flesh, pit

Eat the dark purple varieties to summon the unexpected. The plum is a great fruit to work with when you want to be surprised or turn a new corner in your life. Dry and carry the pit as a talisman for spontaneity in life.

Poke

RULER: Saturn
TYPE: plant
MAGICKAL FORM: root

Carry the poke root to break a hex or curse placed upon you. This should alleviate symptoms immediately. Sprinkle the powdered root outside a home to confuse those who plot against you. This is especially useful when dealing with difficult and unfriendly neighbors.

Pomegranate

RULER: Persephone, Astarte
TYPE: fruit
MAGICKAL FORM: seeds, juice, outer skin

Two strong traditions surround the pomegranate. In Wicca, it is the sacred fruit of Persephone and represents her journey into the underworld. Much superstition revolves around the eating of the fruit. It is customary to eat three seeds on Samhain (Halloween) in remembrance of her journey; eating more than that is believed to bring hardship into the coming year. The second tradition stems from the Middle East where the fruit symbolizes wealth and fertility. Here the custom is to eat as much as possible in order to bring prosperity into the life. The pomegranate juice symbolizes the menstrual or wise blood of the goddess; to drink it is to gain her wisdom. Carry a dried piece of the outer skin or added it to spells for conception.

Poplar

RULER: Saturn
TYPE: plant
MAGICKAL FORM: buds

Carry poplar buds with you when seeking employment. Crush and add them to traditional money incense when you work on commission and need to attract more funds. The poplar buds may also be added to divination blends and make a great ingredient for psychics wishing to attract more business, as well as improving their powers.

Poppet (aka Voodoo Dolls)

RULER: Moon
TYPE: doll
MAGICKAL FORM: cloth, potato

The earliest poppets were carved out of potatoes. Later on elaborate cloth dolls were sewn to serve as sympathetic representations of people. Poppets, or voodoo dolls, can be used to heal and also to hex. Use them in love magick, marriage, and weight-loss spells. Traditionally, the poppet must contain something belonging to the person it represents. Use a lock of hair, a fingernail clipping, saliva, or any bodily fluid. Or glue a picture of the person onto the face of the doll.

Poppy

RULER: Neptune
TYPE: plant
MAGICKAL FORM: flower

The opiate of flowers, the poppy has hallucinogenic powers. It is used to make opium and heroine. Use the petals of the flower—it's legal—to create a dreamy effect. Bathe in the flowers to make yourself mesmerizing.

Potato

RULER: Moon
TYPE: root vegetable
MAGICKAL FORM: raw, cooked

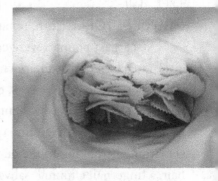

The first voodoo dolls were made from potatoes. This vegetable is a great choice for positive sympathetic magick as it holds great properties of healing and protection. For weight-loss spells, the potato must not be eaten. Carve your name into the potato and peel it during a waning moon while visualizing losing weight. Eat *mashed potatoes* for comfort. Eat potato chips for grounding and protection.

Pretzel

RULER: Sun
TYPE: food
MAGICKAL FORM: knotted

The traditional pretzel is shaped in the form of a Celtic or solar cross. It is a sacred symbol and highly protective. Eat three salted knotted pretzels on a Sunday to protect yourself from harm during the coming week.

Prune

RULER: Sun
TYPE: fruit
MAGICKAL FORM: dried

Eat the dried plum for endurance and add it to anti-aging, preservation, or beauty spells. The prune also loosens the restrictive influence of Saturn; eat some when you feel you have too many difficult obstacles in your life.

Pumpkin

RULER: Oshun, Hecate
TYPE: fruit
MAGICKAL FORM: flesh, seeds

Hollowed and carved on Halloween, pumpkins become jack-o'-lanterns used to honor the spirits of the dead. The pump-

kin also protects the living from harm from any baneful spirits. This fruit is also sacred to the Yoruban goddess Oshun and is offered to her in exchange for wishes granted concerning love, money, and fertility. Offer whole pumpkins smeared with honey to the river when you wish to conceive a child. Offer whole pumpkins with names carved into them for love spells. Throw a handful of pumpkin seeds into the river and ask for a financial boon. It is important to know that the pumpkin and its seeds are considered the children of Oshun. If you are working with her magick, you must abstain from eating any pumpkin.

Purple

RULER: Oya, Jupiter
TYPE: color
MAGICKAL FORM: candles, cloth

This is the color of power, influence, prophecy, and wisdom. Burn purple candles to increase business. It is also a great color for those pursuing higher education. Use purple candles in love spells to make a partner stay at home and remain faithful. Purple altar cloths are the best choice for psychic work or to wrap up tarot cards.

Purselane

RULER: Moon
TYPE: herb
MAGICKAL FORM: shoots

Often considered nothing more than a weed, purselane has many magickal properties. Soldiers should carry a sprig to protect themselves on the battlefield. Add to a bath or floor wash to get rid of evil influences. Eat in green salads to increase your income and protect your assets.

Q

Quadrant (or Quarter)

RULER: four elements
TYPE: directions
MAGICKAL FORM: east, south, west, north

To cast a witches' circle, you must invoke the four quarters. The witch walks clockwise beginning in either the east or the north, saluting each direction and finally returning to the original point to complete the circle. Each quadrant rules a different element and area of life. To be more successful with spells, set up an altar in the quadrant that complements your work. The east rules air and thought; this is the realm of psychic exploration. The south rules fire, drive, and passion; sex or energy magick are best worked in this quarter. It is also the place to find motivation or drive. The west rules water and the emotions; work love magick and healing here. The north is earth and the best place for money magick or anything that requires physical manifestation.

Quartz Crystal

RULER: Earth
TYPE: mineral
MAGICKAL FORM: polished, unpolished

Use this mineral for healing and channeling. All crystals should be cleansed in saltwater for three days before initial use and rinsed with saltwater or charged with sunlight between each use. Place them on body parts that need healing or arrange them in a circle around a photograph of a sick

person. Crystals open lines of communication and improve channeling of spirits. Keep crystals in a room to give you more mental clarity and improve your memory. Use *double terminated* crystals or ones with points on both ends to send psychic messages. *Herkimer diamonds* are tiny quartz crystals mined in upstate New York; carry them for energy, creativity, and originality, or place them under your pillow to help remember your dreams.

Queen of the Meadow

RULER: Hecate
TYPE: herb
MAGICKAL FORM: dried

Add some to bathwater or sprinkle on top of any tool of divination (tarot cards, crystal balls, runes, etc.) to see the future.

Quicksilver, *see* Mercury

Quince

RULER: Venus
TYPE: fruit
MAGICKAL FORM: seed, fruit

The Romans offered quince in the temple of Venus to petition the goddess for happiness in love. Place a quince on a love altar with a white or pink cloth and surround with seven red candles to safeguard and strengthen your love relationship. Carry quince seeds for protection while traveling.

Radish

RULER: Mars
TYPE: vegetable
MAGICKAL FORM: red, white

Eat salted *red* radishes to protect a love relationship, or salted *white* radishes for spiritual protection. Dry radish roots and add to floor wash or bathwater to drive away fear and increase your ambition.

Rain

RULER: Moon, Jupiter
TYPE: water
MAGICKAL FORM: first rainwater collected at beginning of
the four seasons

Collect the first *spring rainwater* and add it to love baths to
attract a new partner. It is a great way to cleanse and renew
yourself before opening your heart to love again. Use *summer
rainwater* for lust spells, *fall rainwater* for charisma, and *winter
rainwater* for courage, power, and endurance. Stand under a
rainbow and make a wish for creativity or inspiration.

Raisin

RULER: crone goddesses
TYPE: fruit
MAGICKAL FORM: dried

Sun-drying grapes produces this small, shriveled fruit. Eat
for wisdom and longevity. Raisins are great to eat on birth-
days, as they help you to age gracefully.

Raspberry

RULER: Venus
TYPE: fruit
MAGICKAL FORM: dried, fresh

Eat fresh raspberries to invoke fun and playfulness. They
are great for turning around a relationship that is getting too
heavy or serious. Eat dried raspberries or carry them for protection. Raspberries tone down fears and promote bravery.

Rattles

RULER: South American deities
TYPE: instrument
MAGICKAL FORM: various

Use a gourd filled with seeds or a rattle to chase away negative energy. Keep one on the altar and shake before any magickal work to clear the air. Weather magick uses rattles, mostly to bring rain.

Rattlesnake Root

RULER: Hermes
TYPE: herb
MAGICKAL FORM: root

Carry the root in the pocket to attract money. It's particularly useful for salesmen or anyone who works on commission or travels with his work.

Red

RULER: Mars, Venus
TYPE: color
MAGICKAL FORM: candle, cloth, visualization of the color

This is the color of lust, passion, and deep abiding love. It is also the color of blood and bonding. Visualize the color red for energy and healing and also for protection.

Rhodochrosite

RULER: Venus
TYPE: mineral
MAGICKAL FORM: gemstone

Wear it to open centers of compassion and humility. This stone helps with emotional expression and attracts harmony and friendship into your life.

Rhubarb

RULER: Erzuli
TYPE: vegetable
MAGICKAL FORM: stalk

Cook and serve this vegetable to keep a mate faithful. Rhubarb is the antidivorce ingredient that's used to solve domestic problems. Sweeten and feed to children to protect them and bring happiness into their lives.

Rice

RULER: Sun, Buddha
TYPE: grain
MAGICKAL FORM: cooked, raw

In Eastern mythology, rice is believed to have a soul just like humans. It is one of the most spiritual grains and should never be wasted. Carry *raw rice* grains for protection. We traditionally throw raw rice over a married couple to bless them with fertility. (Rice is harmful to birds, so birdseed is a safer substitute.) For a marriage spell, place a picture of a couple in a jar and pour a cup of rice on top. Then add the peel of whole orange or orange blossom oil and seal the lid with wax drippings of a pink candle. Finally, place the jar under the bed and shake once a night until you are offered a marriage proposal. Cooked *jasmine rice* empowers your sexuality.

Roots

RULER: Earth
TYPE: plant
MAGICKAL FORM: whole

Voodoo, southern magick, and Wicca all employ roots for spellwork. They are used to ground, center, and pull energy and physical manifestation toward the possessor. Carry roots for power, luck, money, protection, and love.

Rose

RULER: Venus, Oshun, Taurus
TYPE: flower
MAGICKAL FORM: flowers, oil, thorn

This scent is generally worn as a perfume to attract love. Often the dried flowers are added to success formulas. This flower is always a good choice to adorn your love altar. Keep the flowers fresh and change them every Friday. Use *white roses* for cleansing and to heal problems in love. Use *yellow roses* for friendship, though they can also denote jealousy if not given by a true friend. The Yoruban goddess Oshun loves these flowers. Float five (or any multiple of five) fresh yellow roses in a river and ask Oshun to fulfill a wish concerning fame, wealth, admiration, or love. Promise to give her more after she fulfills your request. *Red roses* symbolize passion and true love. Drink a tea of dried red rosebuds to increase your passion. Prepare a bath with red rose petals and a cup of rosewater or three drops of rose oil to infuse your aura with sexuality.

Rose Geranium

RULER: Moon
TYPE: flower
MAGICKAL FORM: oil, flower

This is one of the best scents for emotional cleansing and healing a broken heart. Add a few drops to your bathwater on a Monday to help you let go of a failed relationship.

Rosehips

RULER: Sun
TYPE: plant
MAGICKAL FORM: seeds

Eat some to lift your spirits and promote good health. Add rosehips to money spells to find a job that makes you happy.

Rosemary

RULER: Jupiter, Hecate
TYPE: herb
MAGICKAL FORM: fresh sprigs, dried powder, oil

A favorite herb of witches, rosemary also has a long history of being used to counteract bad spells and block their powers.

Hang fresh or dried sprigs of rosemary in your home to dispel witchcraft and evil plots. Carry the leaves in a red cloth bag for protection. Season food with dried ground rosemary to improve your memory and increase your clarity. Rub the oil into yellow candles and light on a Thursday to improve your study habits and grades.

Rose of Jericho

RULER: Christ
TYPE: plant
MAGICKAL FORM: flower

Also called the miraculous rose, this flower restores hope and brings renewal, prosperity, and immortality. When placed in water, the brown dried flower turns green and comes back to life. Keep in a bowl of water on the altar and refresh the water every Sunday. Regular use prevents depression and despondency and creates more possibilities in any area of your life.

Rose Quartz

RULER: Venus
TYPE: mineral
MAGICKAL FORM: polished or unpolished

Carry this gemstone near the heart to fulfill your desires in love. Hold to calm fears and alleviate loneliness. Place on top of a picture of someone you are quarreling with to overcome anger and open his or her heart to forgive you.

Rowan

RULER: Sun
TYPE: tree
MAGICKAL FORM: branch, leaves, berries

Place the leaves or berries along window ledges to protect the home. A rowan wand or walking stick will protect you from being harmed on a journey and bring spiritual enlightenment along your path. Make two twigs into the shape of a cross and tie together with red string for serious protection.

Ruby

RULER: Sun
TYPE: mineral
MAGICKAL FORM: raw, polished stone

This is the stone of leadership and personal integrity. Wear a ruby to increase your passion and drive in life. It adds depth and longevity to love relationships when both members of the couple wear or carry one.

Rue

RULER: Hecate, Diana
TYPE: herb
MAGICKAL FORM: dried leaves, oil

Known as the queen of the herbs, rue has many magickal properties. Add drops of the oil or a handful of the herb to bathwater to restore your health. Mix the dried herb in a bowl of spring water and sprinkle around a home to bring peaceful vibrations or remove a jinx. For conquest, charm, attraction, and love carry the herb in a red cloth bag next to your heart. Burn dried rue and green candles rubbed with rue oil on a full moon to summon prosperity.

Rum

RULER: Ellegua, Chango
TYPE: alcohol
MAGICKAL FORM: dark, clear, extract

Distilled from molasses and caramel, rum has a deep brown color that attracts sweetness; drinking it channels the spirits of the gods. Rum is also given as an offering to attract their favor. Traditionally, you must spit the rum over an idol or representation of the god. Or spit it over candles (white or red) to enhance the energy of the candles.

Rutabaga

RULER: Venus
TYPE: vegetable
MAGICKAL FORM: roots

Eat rutabaga when you want to maintain power in a situation. Wrap a piece of the root around the left ankle to gain entry into exclusive circles. It's great for social climbers.

Rye

RULER: Mercury
TYPE: herb
MAGICKAL FORM: seed

Add rye or caraway seeds to your diet to evoke your sense of humor. Place the seeds under the tongue to improve your wit and cleverness in communication.

S

Saffron

RULER: Jupiter, Oshun
TYPE: spice
Form: dried

An herb of both spiritual and material wealth, saffron opens channels for happiness and fulfillment. Its powers of divination are quite strong. Drink in a tea to increase psychic vibration. Stain hands and feet in ritual to change your fortune for the better. Cook with rice for joy and prosperity.

Sage

RULER: Sun, Native American gods
TYPE: plant
MAGICKAL FORM: loose, wands

One of the strongest purifying agents, sage is used to drive out evil. Burn it to clear a space of negativity or just to prepare it for any sacred purpose. Pass crystals through the smoke of sage to clean them. Smudge your body with sage for healing and cleansing or add sage as seasoning to food for internal purification.

Saint-John's-wort

RULER: Moon
TYPE: herb
MAGICKAL FORM: powdered, tincture

This herb cures depression and symptoms of PMS when taken internally. But it's not recommended for use while taking birth control pills.

Salt

RULER: Earth
TYPE: mineral
MAGICKAL FORM: coarse, fine

Sacred to all ocean deities and considered one of the most sacred substances of the earth, salt represents prosperity. It was once used to pay salaries in ancient Rome: the word *salary* comes from the Latin *sal*, for salt. Add some to dark leafy greens to increase your income. *Sea salt* is sacred to all ocean deities and used for cleansing. Sprinkle around the four corners of the room and add to baths to protect and dispel evil. Many superstitions arose around spilling salt because of its preciousness. In Wicca, salt is sprinkled to purify and create the sacred circle. Sprinkle *black salt* on doorways to keep away undesirable influences.

Saltpeter

RULER: Mars
TYPE: salt
MAGICKAL FORM: used in fire magick

Found in cigarette papers and once fed to prison inmates to decrease their sex drive, saltpeter is used in ritual for purification. The pure form is available in traditional occult shops. Mix with chamomile and saffron and throw into a fire or hot coal in a cauldron to elevate your consciousness and bring spiritual awareness to a higher level.

Sand

RULER: ocean deities
TYPE: mineral
MAGICKAL FORM: dry, wet, colored

On a magickal level, sand represents the multitude of possibilities that exist in our worlds. One grain of sand represents the uniqueness of the individual. A handful of sand represents the great influence yielded by like-minded people. Bring sand into the home when you want to attract a group of people who share your same interests. Place it in a dish and burn your incense on it. Sift sand through the hands to open up possibilities and more options in your life. Build sandcastles to make dreams come true. Wet sand helps to ground and realize potential. Colored sand brings variety to life.

Sandalwood

RULER: Venus, Mercury, Buddha, Moon
TYPE: Herb
MAGICKAL FORM: bark, oil

The bark or oil derived from the *white* variety of sandalwood is extremely sacred and used for purification. It is given as an offering for spiritual guidance. Use the *red* variety for earth magic and money and love requests. Wear sandalwood oil to increase your spiritual awareness and add to other earthy ingredients for lust and riches.

Sangria

RULER: Bacchus, Venus
TYPE: alcoholic beverage
MAGICKAL FORM: white, red

Use sangria in ritual feasting and for libation. The mixture of wine and fruit is said to bring on ecstasy. Drink *white sangria* to find more happiness within yourself. Drink *red sangria* to experience more pleasure and connection with others.

Sardine

RULER: ocean goddesses
TYPE: fish
MAGICKAL FORM: whole

Legend attributes powers of great beauty and seduction to the sardine, which is believed to form the hair of beautiful mermaids. Eat them *smoked* to age well, or with mustard to sharpen your best features. Carry a whole tin in your pocket to capture the attention of beautiful women, but keep it closed or the smell will scare them away.

Sarsaparilla

RULER: Jupiter
TYPE: herb
MAGICKAL FORM: root

Add this root to love or money spells to draw more of either into your life. Submerge the root in your bathwater to attract prosperity and richness in a relationship. Drink sarsaparilla on Thursdays to increase your income. A root carried in the wallet will increase the amount of money in your purse.

Sassafras

RULER: Jupiter
TYPE: plant
MAGICKAL FORM: root

Add to money spells or incense or carry a piece of the root in your wallet. Sassafras is one of the best ingredients for getting out of debt.

Saturday

RULER: Saturn
TYPE: day of the week
MAGICKAL FORM: sunrise, the eighth, sixteenth, and
twenty-fourth hours of the day

A god, goddess, or planet governs each day of the week. It
is easy to spot the ruler of the day by its name. Saturday is the
day for Saturnian magick. You'll have the best results with
spells dealing with work, discipline, power, and conquering
negative conditions on this day. The hour of sunrise and every
eight hours after that are also ruled by Saturn; that makes
these times of the day doubly blessed. These four hours are
the strongest ones to conduct rituals. Check your local newspaper, astrological calendar, or almanac to determine your
local sunrise.

Sauerkraut

RULER: Saturn
TYPE: food
MAGICKAL FORM: warm

Eat sauerkraut for stamina and strength and to help face
your fears of the unknown. Sauerkraut develops character and
builds courage.

Sausage

RULER: Adonis
TYPE: meat
MAGICKAL FORM: whole

This is a phallic food and when cased in the intestinal lining of a sheep it brings luck when eaten. Use sausage for feasting in winter rituals to ward off cold and loneliness.

Scallion

RULER: Mars
TYPE: vegetable
MAGICKAL FORM: raw, cooked

The vegetable is a great cleanser that helps prepare the way for a successful relationship. Eat some when you are getting to know someone to smooth the way and prevent misunderstandings.

Scotch Broom, *see* Broom Tops

Scullcap

RULER: goddess of the hearth
TYPE: herb
MAGICKAL FORM: dried

Drink it in a tea to calm the nerves and bring peace of mind. Add it to a floor wash to create peaceful vibrations in your home. Place some in the left shoe of a vulnerable mate to keep others away from him or her.

Sea Horse

RULER: Venus
TYPE: animal
MAGICKAL FORM: preserved

Sold as a talisman for luck and love, the sea horse leads to understanding and acceptance. It is associated with functional families and emotional well-being.

Seaweed

RULER: Neptune, Venus
TYPE: plant
MAGICKAL FORM: wet, dry

Eat seaweed for prosperity and to discover new sources of income. Scrubbing yourself with seaweed while in the ocean brings good luck and leads to excellent employment opportunities.

Seltzer (or Sparkling Water)

RULER: Mercury
TYPE: water
MAGICKAL FORM: orange or lime flavored

Drink seltzer or add it to bathwater to stimulate creativity and popularity. *Orange*-flavored seltzer brings excitement to your love life. *Lime*-flavored seltzer will help others notice you and appreciate your work.

Senna

RULER: Saturn
TYPE: plant
MAGICKAL FORM: pods

To loosen restrictions in life and overcome obstacles, work with senna pods in ritual. If taken internally, they will also loosen the bowels.

Sesame

RULER: Sun
TYPE: plant
MAGICKAL FORM: seed, oil

Sprinkle sesame seeds, an all-around prosperity food, on greens to greatly improve your income and increase your happiness. The seeds are also used in fertility rites to increase male sperm count and in sex spells to reach ecstatic states. Burn *black sesame seeds* to dispel evil and nightmares. After having a bad dream or whenever you feel negative energy in the home, take a spoonful of black sesame seeds and cradle them in a piece of tinfoil fashioned into a small bowl or cup shape. Place the foil directly over the burner on the stove. (Gas is best but electric will work, too.) Turn up the heat until the sesame seeds begin to smoke. Continue heating until they catch on fire. Once the seeds are on fire, turn off the heat and let them burn until they extinguish. This blesses the home and removes bad vibes. It is also traditional to burn them in a pot that can be carried around through all the rooms of the home and to pass the smoking pot around an individual to cleanse and protect him or her.

Seven-Color Candles

RULER: Orishas
TYPE: wax
MAGICKAL FORM: candle in glass

Place a seven-color candle in a glass and burn it to honor the seven orishas (deities) in Santeria. They are also burned to remove overall obstacles in life. Use one when just about everything seems to be going wrong. Meditate upon the areas associated with each color as the candle burns. These candles are always found in good occult shops and botanicas and work quickly. You will notice immediate results.

Shallot

RULER: Mars
TYPE: herb
MAGICKAL FORM: cooked, raw

Eat shallots or place in some in the bathwater for healing after a traumatic experience. Shallots ward off negative situations and keep one from repeating negative patterns.

Shoes

RULER: Earth
TYPE: various
MAGICKAL FORM: various

Much superstition surrounds wearing shoes of the dead because it is believed that by doing so you may absorb bad karma. However, walking or stepping in another living person's shoes is a symbolic way to understand his path. Shoes lead the way and deliver us safely on our journey. Always shine the shoes and add spit before embarking on a new endeavor to gain confidence. Sex and love magick also uses shoes. Put your hand in a woman's shoe to have success with her in the bedroom. Sprinkle cumin powder into shoes to keep a lover faithful. Do the same with protective herbs in the shoes of children to keep them out of harm's way.

Silk

RULER: Earth
TYPE: fabric
MAGICKAL FORM: various colors

Wrap your tarot cards in silk, as it's one of the best fabrics available for protecting your psychic tools from being infiltrated by spirits of confusion. Those who cover their tools or altars with it will be able to interpret omens without doubt. Silk is also great for making dream pillows as it creates deep relaxation. Use it (instead of cotton) to make love ouanga bags when you want someone to treat you extra special. Silk brings a touch of extravagance to any ritual.

Silver

RULER: Moon
TYPE: mineral
MAGICKAL FORM: metal, color, candle

This color increases psychic vibrations. Burn silver candles to honor the goddess. Talismans made out of silver are very protective. Keep silver coins on an altar to bring a positive change in fortune.

Skunk Cabbage

RULER: Saturn
TYPE: plant
MAGICKAL FORM: dried

Carry a pinch of this plant in the pocket to improve your reputation. Sprinkle skunk cabbage around a black candle and burn it to stop gossip and slander.

Slippery Elm

RULER: Mercury
TYPE: plant
MAGICKAL FORM: lozenges, powder

Besides curing a sore throat, slippery elm, when ingested or held under the tongue, improves speech and communication. It adds eloquence and clarity to your speech.

Snail

RULER: Venus
TYPE: sea animal
MAGICKAL FORM: shell

Place a snail on the altar to slow things down. It is a great talisman for making a successful situation last. Eating snails induces lust.

Snakeroot

RULER: Saturn
TYPE: plant
MAGICKAL FORM: root

Carry the root of this plant as a luck and money talisman. Add it to bathwater when you need to "snake" your way into a position. It's great for maneuvering your way up in political or business situations.

Snakeskin

RULER: Asclepious, Lilith
TYPE: animal skin
MAGICKAL FORM: whole, piece

Add a piece of shed snakeskin to money or healing oils. Keep a whole shed snakeskin in a coil or spiral roll on an altar to invoke power for the magician or healer.

Snapdragon

RULER: Mercury
TYPE: flower
MAGICKAL FORM: fresh

Bring this flower into the workplace for inspiration. Snapdragons drive the blues away and make work more fun. They can also be snapped or broken to break a hex or cut through any negative energy being sent your way.

Snow

RULER: Freya
TYPE: water
MAGICKAL FORM: frozen, melted

Bury a piece of paper in the snow with a wish for something you want to hold or freeze in place. This is a great spell for anyone wishing to maintain a title or honor. It will stop your competition from achieving success. If snow is not available, bury the paper in crushed ice and place in the freezer. Also, use snow to melt down a hard heart. Write the name of someone who is angry with you or cold hearted toward you and stick the paper in a bowl of fresh snow. (You can also use ice cubes.) Pour boiling water over the snow until it melts. Sprinkle this water around a picture of this person or across a path he is sure to tread.

Sodalite

RULER: Mercury
TYPE: mineral
MAGICKAL FORM: raw, polished

This stone of truthfulness is especially effective when brought into court to force someone to tell the truth. Wear the stone around people who constantly argue. It will clear up their thinking and create more positive communication.

Solomon's Seal

RULER: Mercury
TYPE: plant
MAGICKAL FORM: oil, root

To gain wisdom or prophetic sight, place the root under the pillow while you sleep. Anoint a purple candle with the oil to have success in court. Add Solomon's seal to money spells when you want to bring in millions. It is an herb of great wealth. Rub some into yellow candles to protect your fortune or assets.

Sorrel

RULER: Venus
TYPE: plant
MAGICKAL FORM: leaves

Place some leaves in a sick room to give the patient some healing energy. Sorrel strengthens the spiritual immune system and is one of the best herbs to use during emotional or physical recovery from illness.

Southernwood

RULER: Jupiter
TYPE: plant
MAGICKAL FORM: powder, cut bark

Burn the bark to strengthen family bonds and drive away unwanted influences in the home. Add some to house-blessing formulas to keep peaceful vibrations.

Soy

RULER: Moon
TYPE: vegetable
MAGICKAL FORM: beans, tofu, soy sauce

Sacred to ancient Chinese and Japanese agricultural deities, soy carries a very high spiritual vibration. Sprinkle the beans on the ground outside the home to honor and appease the dead, or just carry some in your pocket for good luck. Season food of any type with soy sauce to add a protective element. For example, adding soy sauce to dark greens will protect your income, or add to tomatoes to protect your love relationship. Eat tofu for good health. It also increases psychic awareness and protection when eaten on a full moon.

Spanish Moss

RULER: Jupiter
TYPE: plant
MAGICKAL FORM: fresh, dried

Grow around your home to protect and build your financial assets. Add the dried moss to money incense to give new life to your business.

Spearmint, *see* Mint

Spelt

RULER: Mercury
TYPE: wheat
MAGICKAL FORM: flour, bread, pasta

Eat spelt as a quick fix to financial problems. Sprinkle the flour across coins on an altar to make your money last longer. This is a great ingredient for those looking for discipline to stay on a budget.

Spikenard

RULER: Mary
TYPE: plant
MAGICKAL FORM: oil, ointment

Associated with holiness and spiritual enlightenment, spikenard provides spiritual assistance when rubbed onto white candles. Apply some on the third eye to gain insight and wisdom about your path or purpose in life. Spikenard also relieves feelings of guilt and lifts burdens or depression.

Spinach

RULER: Jupiter
TYPE: vegetable
MAGICKAL FORM: raw, steamed

Eat spinach raw to increase physical energy, good health, and fortune. Steam and eat some on a full moon to increase your income. This is a fast-working ingredient and always brings positive results.

Spit

RULER: various
TYPE: body fluid
MAGICKAL FORM: your own, another's

Every culture has a myth about spit and spitting. According to one North American legend, the earth was created from snot and spit. In eastern Europe, spitting three times over your shoulder wards off the evil eye. Use spit to seal pacts and bind oaths. In Wicca, one's own spit added to ouanga bags seals them with power. Spit is also an identifying signature to let the spirits know who should be the recipient of good fortune. Collect the saliva of another person for love magick. The easiest way to accomplish this is to take the end of a straw or cigarette butt he has sucked upon and burn it along with herbs and oils of love.

Sponge

RULER: Moon, Venus
TYPE: real, synthetic
MAGICKAL FORM: sea sponge, kitchen sponge

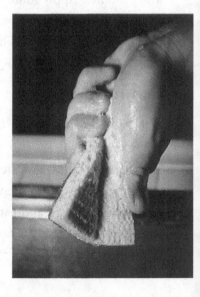

Use *organic* or *sea sponges*, such as a loofah, for beauty and love spells. Take into an herbal bath and scrub the skin for beauty or to infuse your aura with charm. *Synthetic sponges* cleanse negative energy and release anger. Anyone who works with distressed or troubled persons should do sponge cleansings on a daily basis. Take a clean sponge and run water over it. Squeeze the sponge out with your hands and visualize letting go of anger or any pain that you have absorbed. Repeat three times. This ritual is very good for psychotherapists and psychic counselors. It can also be used by anyone who easily absorbs the negative energy of another.

Squash

RULER: Sun, Native American gods
TYPE: vegetable
MAGICKAL FORM: whole, cooked

Known as the sustaining sister in Native American lore, squash is the ally and friend in a time of need. Place a whole decorative squash on an altar to draw friendly assistance into your life. Eat squash to bond more deeply with friends, family, or lovers. It's a great ingredient to work with when you need people to be on your side.

Squill

RULER: Saturn
TYPE: plant
MAGICKAL FORM: root

Sprinkle shavings from the root in a circle around a green candle to protect your assets during divorce proceedings, or around a black or brown candle to get someone off your back.

Star Anise, see Anise

Stone

RULER: Earth
TYPE: mineral
MAGICKAL FORM: various

Smooth rocks or stones kept near moving water (behind the toilet, for example) bring prosperity to the home. Carry black, white, or speckled stones or place them on an altar for good luck. Wear a stone with a hole in it for protection.

Straw, Grain

RULER: Sun
TYPE: plant
MAGICKAL FORM: hay

Stuff voodoo dolls with hay to attract spirits. A straw broom brings good luck when used to sweep a house.

Straw, Tube

RULER: Venus
TYPE: drinking implement
MAGICKAL FORM: paper, metal

In Argentina and Uruguay, a metal straw called a *bombilla* is used to drink hot tea or maté. This straw blesses a union when shared by two lovers. Use *paper* straws to obtain the saliva of someone you wish to cast a love spell upon. Cut the tip of the straw and add it to love herbs to create the desired effects.

Strawberry

RULER: Erzuli, Venus
TYPE: fruit
MAGICKAL FORM: fresh,
dried

Flirtatious and fun,
strawberries can also stir
things up and cause a lot of trouble. They are used in spells to
attract an extramarital affair or to force a change in partners.

String

RULER: Arachne, Fortuna
TYPE: cloth
MAGICKAL FORM: red, black

All binding rituals require string. Use *red string* for love
and *black string* to stop enemies. Tie a doll or human figure
candle with seven or nine knots to create the binding. Wear
red string around your wrist or ankle to ward off the evil eye.

Styrax

RULER: Mercury
TYPE: plant
MAGICKAL FORM: resin, oil

This is one of the most pleasing scents to offer to the god
Mercury. He will immediately come to your aid when you use
styrax. Burn as incense or rub the oil onto orange candles and
light on his altar. Wear styrax to remove obstacles.

Sugar

RULER: Orishas, Venus
TYPE: plant
MAGICKAL FORM: powdered, raw, cane, liquid, confectioners'

The sweet cane reed is sacred to many of the Cuban, Brazilian, and African gods and offered to win their favors. Chew on raw sugar cane to draw spirits into the body; it is one of the quickest ways to become possessed by the gods. Sprinkle *powdered* or *confectioners'* sugar on pink or red love candles to make another "sweet" on you. All refined sugar brings quick magickal results but it also has some negative karma associated with it unless it is used in the purely raw form. You can always expect some hidden clause to show up when sugar is used for love spells. Many practitioners feel the "high interest" is worth the price to quickly obtain their heart's desire. Sugar substitutes have no magickal qualities.

Sulfur

RULER: Saturn, Vulcan, Hecate
TYPE: chemical
MAGICKAL FORM: yellow powder, match head

One of the three sacred ingredients of the alchemists, sulfur, or brimstone, is used for physical and spiritual transformation, to get rid of negative energy, and also for hexing. Sulfur powder can be found in proper occult supply shops. To remove a particularly strong presence of evil, burn a small pinch of sulfur on a charcoal briquette in a cauldron. Sprinkle sulfur powder around the outside of a dwelling to get rid of negativity. Match heads also contain sulfur and lighting three matches in one strike will clear a room and prepare it for spiritual work. To get rid of something wicked sent your way, light a match and inhale the sulfur fumes. To eliminate a nasty individual, fill a small bottle or jar with one-third salt and one-third red pepper. Add nine match heads (or powdered sulfur) to the jar and insert a piece of paper with the name of an enemy written on it into the jar. Shake the jar nine times a day for nine days. After the ninth day, seal the jar by dripping the wax of a black or brown candle around the lid. Then dispose of the jar at least nine miles away from your house or place of work. This person will disappear from your life within nine days to nine weeks.

Sunday

RULER: Sun
TYPE: day of the week
MAGICKAL FORM: sunrise, the eighth, sixteenth, and twenty-fourth hours of the day

A god, goddess, or planet governs each day of the week. It is easy to spot the ruler of the day by its name. Sunday is the day of the Sun, and favors magick for love, happiness, health, and wealth. The hour of sunrise will be the most powerful time to work, especially if you want to infuse energy into your work. Sunset is the second best time and is favored when you need to calm down a situation. Check your local newspaper, astrological calendar, or almanac to determine time of sunrise and sunset.

Sunflower

RULER: Sun
TYPE: plant
MAGICKAL FORM: flower, seed

Always include a sunflower or sunflower seeds in a birthday spell to increase happiness, health, and years. Sprinkle the seeds on the earth to invoke prosperity. Place the flowers on a love altar to invoke a long-lasting relationship.

Sushi

RULER: Neptune, Venus
TYPE: fish
MAGICKAL FORM: raw

Eating raw fish increases psychic awareness and sexual prowess. Combined with seaweed and rice, sushi brings good fortune.

Sweetgrass

RULER: Great Spirit
TYPE: grass
MAGICKAL FORM: braids

This sacred Native American grass is burned to bring good and beneficial spirits. It is customary to burn it after smudging with cedar and sage, which drives away the negative spirits. It is believed that prayers or wishes are carried to the heavens in the smoke of the sweetgrass.

Sweetpea

RULER: Venus
TYPE: flower
MAGICKAL FORM: flower, oil

Work with this flower or oil to increase your vulnerability and openness. Sweetpea helps to break down emotional barriers and walls of defense. It is a great ingredient for lonely people who shut themselves off from others. Use to attract friends who are trustworthy.

Swiss Chard

RULER: Saturn
TYPE: vegetable
MAGICKAL FORM: steamed

Eat some on Saturdays to help you gain employment. Or consume some on Tuesdays to increase your earnings or get an edge over your competition.

Sword

RULER: air
TYPE: metal
MAGICKAL FORM: double-edged

"Whoever holds the sword, rules the circle," according to a witches' saying. Traditionally the high priestess or high priest holds the coven's one and only sword. Many ceremonial magicians own their own swords, as it is required in their rituals. The sword is used to draw the magick circle and is needed in initiation rites. It must have a double edge and it represents the power of the magician, priestess, or priest.

$\mathcal{T}$

Tamarind

RULER: Astarte
TYPE: plant
MAGICKAL FORM: seeds, pod

Used in ancient Syria as an aphrodisiac and to induce lust, tamarind brings out your wild side. Offer a whole pod to the goddess on your love altar or carry the seeds to make you irresistible.

Tamarisk

RULER: Pan, Cernunos
TYPE: tree
MAGICKAL FORM: leaves, branches

The salt-cedar or tamarisk tree was used by the ancient Mediterranean cultures to drive away bad spirits. Lightly pelt walls or bodies with the branches for an exorcism or cleansing of evil. Carry the leaves for shelter from any spiritual storm.

Tangerine

RULER: Hermes
TYPE: fruit
MAGICKAL FORM: flesh, peel

Dry the peel and add to love spells to invoke a lover who is also a true friend. Eat one to improve your mood or spray the fragrance in a room to create a cheerful relaxing atmosphere.

Tansy

RULER: Venus
TYPE: plant
MAGICKAL FORM: flowers

Drink tansy tea to lengthen your life. Add the flower to any ritual calling for immortality. Tansy can be applied to fertility rituals designed to extend your lineage and it is also a good choice for artists who want to live on through their work.

Tarragon

RULER: Mercury
TYPE: plant
MAGICKAL FORM: fresh sprigs, powdered

Add this "herb of communication" to success formulas and love healing recipes. Spice food with tarragon and eat before a test to get a good grade. Eat some before a big meeting where you are required to make a sales pitch. It's a great choice for those in advertising.

Tea

RULER: Mars
TYPE: plant
MAGICKAL FORM: green, black

Brew a cup of *green* tea and drink while visualizing receiving monies you are owed. Green tea is also good for health and vigor. Add loose *black* tea to protection formulas for strength, or to love spells to increase sexual desire.

Tea Tree

RULER: Mercury
TYPE: plant
MAGICKAL FORM: oil

Rub some oil into the skin to relax your muscles and promote healing and positive vibes. A drop of tea tree oil under the tongue promotes conversation and helps to break the ice with strangers.

Tears

RULER: Moon
TYPE: water
MAGICKAL FORM: fresh

Drum up some tears while working a spell to get a lover to come back. Let them fall freely into your potion and mix well. The love gods are very partial to tears and suffering of the heart. Tears will make them answer your requests quickly. In general, petitioning for anything with heartfelt tears makes the gods more open to answering your prayers.

Teeth

RULER: Saturn
TYPE: human, animal
MAGICKAL FORM: carried in pouch, worn or placed under pillow

Talismans of power, luck, and protection are often made with teeth. They are added to Native American medicine bags and carried to attract spirits to guide one on the journey of life. The teeth of wolves, snakes, bears, and oxen are the most popular. *Baby teeth* attract money when placed under a pillow. Carry a molar to gain wisdom and insight.

Thistle

RULER: Mars
TYPE: plant
MAGICKAL FORM: living plant, cutting

Grow some in a garden to protect the home from thieves.

Carry a piece as a defense against psychic or real attack. Thistle is one of the best herbs to carry when involved in magickal wars. It prevents hexes and curses from taking place. *Holy thistle* is used for purification and to get rid of guilty feelings. Pregnant women should carry *milk thistle* to keep their partners from cheating.

Thorn

RULER: Venus
TYPE: plant
MAGICKAL FORM: thorn from a red rose

Use a thorn to prick the left thumb and draw blood. Then add the blood to a love potion to keep a lover faithful. Add seven crushed thorns to powdered rose petals and jasmine flowers to catch a mate you suspect of cheating.

Thread

RULER: Arachne
TYPE: cotton, silk, various colors
MAGICKAL FORM: spooled, knotted, sewn

Use thread in knot magick, binding spells, and protection rituals. It is also used to sew ouanga bags. Thread represents the weaving of fate. Visualize a clear picture of the desired future outcome whenever working with thread.

Thunderbolt

RULER: Thor
TYPE: image
MAGICKAL FORM: real, symbolic

Sigils of thunderbolts are carved into candles to increase the power of the spell. The image is cast in silver or gold and worn to empower the magician. When a real thunderbolt (lightning) is seen, make a wish concerning power.

Thursday

RULER: Thor, Jupiter
TYPE: day of the week
MAGICKAL FORM: sunrise, the eighth, sixteenth, and twenty-fourth hours of the day

A god, goddess, or planet governs each day of the week. It is easy to spot the ruler of the day by its name. In the word *Thursday*, we see the roots of the name of the Norse god Thor. In Spanish, this day of the week is called Jueves and derived from Jove or Jupiter. Work magick for wisdom, money, and protection on Thursdays. Keep in mind that Jupiter magick always makes more of whatever you have. So if you have nothing, this is not the best energy to work with. The hour of sunrise and every eight hours after that are also ruled by Jupiter, and that makes these times of the day doubly blessed. These four hours are the strongest ones to do ritual in. Check your local newspaper, astrological calendar, or almanac to determine your local sunrise.

Thyme

RULER: fairies, Venus
TYPE: herb
MAGICKAL FORM: fresh, dried, oil

Add this herb to foods to increase your awareness, sight, and memory. Bathe in the oil for serious purification after you have come in contact with death. Thyme cleanses and renews the spirit and calls angelic forces to one's aid. It is also used in love spells to invoke more gentleness and understanding into a relationship.

Tiger's Eye

RULER: Sun
TYPE: mineral
MAGICKAL FORM: cut, polished

Use it to dispel illusions and deception. Tiger's eye protects and strengthens the will of the wearer. It keeps false friends away.

Tinfoil

RULER: Saturn
TYPE: household item
MAGICKAL FORM: reflective side out

This is one of the most magickal modern ingredients. Tin- or aluminum foil makes a better pouch than cloth to hold magickal ingredients because it magnifies their properties and magnetizes the prayer into manifestation. Use it to make ouanga bags. Take a small square, fill with herbs or flowers of your choice, and fold up tightly. Place it in a wallet, or carry it in your pocket or over the heart.

Tobacco

RULER: Mars, Ellegua, Chango, Native American gods
TYPE: loose, cigarettes, cigars, essential oil
MAGICKAL FORM: loose, cigarettes, cigars, essential oil

Blow tobacco smoke to the four directions, and above and below, for purification. Offer *cigar* smoke to Ellegua (who lives behind doorways) as an appeal to open doors. Blow cigar smoke in front of Chango or Santa Barbara statues for business success. Ekkeco is a South American god who resides over the home; keep statues of him in the kitchen and place *cigarettes* in his open mouth along with requests for daily needs. Add *loose tobacco* to love recipes to increase stamina and sex drive. Smoke small amounts of tobacco to induce lust.

Tofu, *see* Soy

Tomato

RULER: Venus
TYPE: vegetable
MAGICKAL FORM: flesh, skin, seeds, dried, fresh

Called the "love apple," the tomato nurtures the "dangerous" or wild side of love. Eat alone to bring out your seductive powers and passion for life. Mix with basil for man/woman love. Use sun-dried tomato with mozzarella balls for gay love, and very juicy tomatoes for lesbian love. Because the tomato is a nightshade, you can also use it for poisonous plots. Crush underfoot while calling out the name of an enemy.

Tonka

RULER: Venus
TYPE: plant
MAGICKAL FORM: beans, oil

The tonka plant is similar to vanilla. Add the beans or oil to love spells to increase pleasure and whet the sexual appetite. Or add some to money or employment spells to lead you toward a job that makes you happy. Use it for both emotional and financial fulfillment.

Topaz

RULER: Sun
TYPE: mineral
MAGICKAL FORM: blue, clear, green, gold, pink

Meditate upon or wear the *blue topaz* for balance, tranquillity, psychic powers, and to strengthen leadership abilities. The *clear topaz* aids with focus, study, and concentration. The *green topaz* brings understanding and emotional healing. The *gold topaz* is for prosperity, happiness, luck, and love. Those seeking the truth or a soul mate should wear a *pink topaz*.

Tourmaline

RULER: Saturn
TYPE: mineral
MAGICKAL FORM: watermelon, green, black

Hold the *black tourmaline* for focus and concentration. The *green tourmaline* attracts new opportunities. Wear the *watermelon tourmaline* during the Saturn return (28½ to 29th year) to ease the grip of the planet and make its lessons more easily integrated. But you can wear it anytime you wish to loosen restrictions in your life.

Tuberose

RULER: Venus
TYPE: flower
MAGICKAL FORM: flower, oil

Used by Aztec healers, the tuberose has a very calming effect when inhaled. Use the oil on pink candles for stress reduction and to heal matters of the heart.

Tuesday

RULER: Mars
TYPE: day of the week
MAGICKAL FORM: sunrise, the eighth, sixteenth, and twenty-fourth hours of the day

A god, goddess, or planet governs each day of the week. It is easy to spot the ruler of the day by its name. The word *Tuesday* is not so easy, but if we look at the word in Spanish, Martes, we clearly see its connection to Mars. This is a day for sex magick, energy, stamina, and health. It is also good for success magick and defense against enemies. On Tuesday, the hour of sunrise and every eight hours after that are also ruled by Mars, and that makes these times of the day doubly blessed. These four hours are the strongest ones to do ritual in. Check your local newspaper, astrological calendar, or almanac to determine your local sunrise.

Tulips

RULER: all fertility goddesses
TYPE: flower
MAGICKAL FORM: fresh

Place *white tulips* on an altar when trying to conceive a child. Use *red tulips* around the home to ensure a healthy delivery. *Yellow tulips* bless both mother and newborn child. *Pink tulips* promote sexual flirtations and are great to use when you want someone else to make the first romantic move.

Turkey

RULER: Great Spirit
TYPE: fowl
MAGICKAL FORM: meat, wishbone, skin

The meat of this bird is eaten for thanksgiving, comfort, and nurturing. When cooked in a home, it brings blessings. When shared with strangers, it brings karmic reward. Eat the skin of the turkey for confidence in love. The breastbone or wishbone is very magickal; pull one between two persons while each makes a wish. The one who pulls off the bigger half will have his or her wish come true.

Turmeric

RULER: Mercury
TYPE: spice
MAGICKAL FORM: powder

Rub the spice (also known as goldenseal) into a phone receiver to keep your phone from being bugged. Or rub some into a white candle and burn it when you want privacy or to ensure that your secrets are being kept. Goldenseal taken internally strengthens the spiritual and physical body.

Turnip

RULER: Saturn
TYPE: vegetable
MAGICKAL FORM: whole, roots

Add a whole turnip to mop water and cleanse the house to keep away unwanted guests. Carry the root of the turnip to ward off dates from hell. It is one of the best ingredients for removing obstacles in your love life.

Turquoise

RULER: Native American deities, Venus, Moon
TYPE: mineral
MAGICKAL FORM: raw, unpolished, set in silver

Wearing this stone brings peace, unity, and respect with nature and other life forms. Set in silver it is very protective and draws love into the life. Turquoise is a stone of honor and poise.

Twilight

RULER: Hecate
TYPE: hour of day
MAGICKAL FORM: at least three stars visible, sun and moon
both visible

Twilight is second to midnight as the most powerful time
to work magick and spells. (Sunrise is the third.) This is called
the time between the worlds and opens the doors to psychic
insight and power. Prayers and requests made during this time
are more likely to be heard and answered.

U

Umbrella

RULER: Moon
TYPE: household item
MAGICKAL FORM: upside down

There are many superstitions about opening an umbrella inside the house. It is true that this brings bad luck, unless the umbrella is opened inverted or with the canopy side down. Use umbrellas in ritual to hold or contain energy or ingredients. Whatever is thrown into the canopy will also multiply. The following is one of the best pieces of umbrella magick. Open the umbrella indoors and upside down. Throw handfuls of raw grains, cedar chips, and crushed bay leaves into the

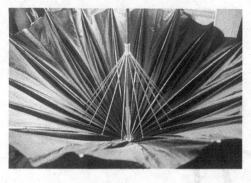

canopy. Spin the canopy clockwise by turning the umbrella handle. Gaze into the spokes and chant your favorite chant eight times. (It should be a chant of prosperity or any goddess or moon chant.) After eight turns and eight chants, snap the umbrella shut. Go outside and open the umbrella correctly with the canopy down over your head. Let yourself be showered with the ingredients to invoke a financial boon.

Unicorn Root

RULER: Moon
TYPE: plant
MAGICKAL FORM: root

Carry the root to keep virginity intact. Add it to love spells to summon a soul mate and also to recall loves from a past life. Unicorn root also renews the soul's innocence. Add it to any recipe where trust is needed.

Urine

RULER: Mars
TYPE: body fluid
MAGICKAL FORM: fresh

Urine is consumed in fasting and purification rituals for cleansing and healing. Add it to protection, cursing, and controlling love spells. Urine is very powerful for marking territory. If you want to obtain a certain property, spread a drop of your urine on the boundaries of the four corners of the land. For apartments and homes, please be civilized with your magick. Simply go to the toilet and pee while you visualize yourself buying or renting the space.

Valerian

RULER: Moon
TYPE: herb
MAGICKAL FORM: powder, tincture

Use this herb in sleeping potions, pain relief, and stress-reduction rituals. It is said that evil spirits do not like the powerful smell of valerian and will be chased away by it. Sniff it to drive away internal demons.

Vanilla

RULER: Venus
TYPE: spice
MAGICKAL FORM: bean, pure
extract, essential oil

Use this scent to increase
the sexual and sensual appetite.
Add the bean to flavor dishes,
or add the pure extract to incense or potpourri and place it
in the bedroom. Vanilla promotes happiness. Wear the oil
as a perfume, or add it to the
bathwater to increase your charms.

Verbena

RULER: Venus
TYPE: plant
MAGICKAL FORM: leaves, oil

Use it alone as a spiritual oil and psychic cleanser. Add it to
cinnamon and patchouli to create a love attraction formula.

Vervain

RULER: Venus, Celtic goddesses
TYPE: herb
MAGICKAL FORM: oil, leaves, powder

This is one of the most sacred fragrances of the Welsh
witches, who wore it or burned it to prepare the way for con-

nection with the God and Goddess. Vervain is the best ingredient to use to wash down an altar or temple before attempting magickal work. It charges the space with power and immediately raises the consciousness of all who enter the space. Use vervain in your protection, love, and immortality spells. Grown on the property, it brings blessings of prosperity to the household. Take vervain baths to prolong your life and renew hope. Dust your hands with the powder to make sure the one you love will love you back.

Vetiver

RULER: Venus, Neptune
TYPE: plant
MAGICKAL FORM: root, grass, powder, oil

This tangled root (also known as khus khus) is added to protection bags and it is believed to "knot up" any enemy who comes against you. Sprinkle the powder or grass in a circle around a purple candle for success and power. Add to money recipes to increase your earning and saving potential. Wear the perfume oil to attract luck in business or love. Rub oil into a brown candle to make a lover stay.

Vinegar

RULER: Saturn
TYPE: condiment, preservative
MAGICKAL FORM: white, red wine, apple cider

Add *apple cider* vinegar to bathwater or drink a teaspoonful a day to prolong your life and maintain good health. Use *white* vinegar in cleansing and purification baths. *Red wine*

vinegar drives thieves away; add it to floor wash to protect a
dwelling.

Violet

RULER: Venus
TYPE: flower
MAGICKAL FORM: flowers, oil

One of the customs surrounding fresh violets is that they
must be stolen or they won't grow. Wild violets increase happiness. Potted violets prevent accidents and soothe the nerves.
This fragrance brings enormous comfort and is used in love
healing spells.

Waffle

RULER: Mercury, Venus
TYPE: bread
MAGICKAL FORM: cooked

The pockets of the waffle are very magickal. Fill them with honey or maple syrup and eat on a new moon to get work that makes you feel happy and satisfied. Fill the pockets with berries and eat on a Friday to draw a more fulfilling love life.

Wahoo Bark

RULER: Pan
TYPE: herb
MAGICKAL FORM: dried bark

This is a hex breaker when used on its own. Sprinkle some around a premise or carry to get rid of a curse. Mix it with sex ingredients sacred to Mars to bring some fireworks into the bedroom.

Wasabi

RULER: Mars
TYPE: spice
MAGICKAL FORM: powdered, sauce

Place a dab of wasabi or hot green mustard under the tongue to open channels and bring clarity. Add the powder to success ouangas with mercurial ingredients to summon more creative drive. This is a great recipe for procrastinators. Eat it with fish for protection.

Water

RULER: ocean and river deities, Venus, Neptune, Moon
TYPE: element
MAGICKAL FORM: baths

The element of water is associated with the western quadrant and represents dreams and feelings. The best way to work with this element is in magickal baths for cleansing, love, healing, protection, and prosperity. Sacred waters include rainwater, spring water, saltwater, holy water, florida water (a special voodoo holy water readily available in occult supply shops), and witches' consecrated water. The best bodies of water to leave offerings in are oceans and rivers.

Watercress

RULER: Mars
TYPE: herb
MAGICKAL FORM: fresh sprigs

Roman soldiers ate watercress to protect themselves in battle. This is one of the best herbs for those serving in the military. Eat steamed or raw watercress on Tuesdays for strength and safety.

Watermelon

RULER: Erzuli
TYPE: fruit
MAGICKAL FORM: fruit, seed, scent

The seeds of the watermelon can provoke infidelity if walked across or swallowed. The seed is sacred to the ocean goddess Yemaya, who rules all aspects of love and married life. Use watermelon to increase luck while gambling. For this, you must eat the flesh while still on the rind.

Wednesday

RULER: Wodin, Mercury
TYPE: day of the week
MAGICKAL FORM: sunrise, the eighth, sixteenth, and twenty-fourth hours of the day

A god, goddess, or planet governs each day of the week. In the Spanish word for Wednesday, *miércoles*, we clearly see its connection to Mercury. The word *Wednesday* is reminiscent of the Norse wind god Wodin, which is referenced in the popular rhyme verse "Wednesday's child is full of woe." This does not mean that those born on this day are full of sorrow or trouble. To be full of Wo (Wodin) means to be full of wind, to be spirited. Woden was such a powerful pagan god that the German church fathers changed the name of his day to Mittwoch, meaning midweek, in an attempt to exorcise his influence. Wednesday is a day for success, creativity, and communication. The hour of sunrise and every eight hours after that are also ruled by Mercury, making these times of the day doubly blessed. These are the strongest four hours for ritual work. Check your local newspaper, astrological calendar, or almanac to determine when sunrise occurs.

Wheat

RULER: Earth Mother, harvest deities
TYPE: grain
MAGICKAL FORM: bread, flour, seed

From ancient times to the present, wheat is one of the most offered gifts to the gods. The Greeks and Romans prepared wheat cakes for temple rituals. Modern pagans offer bread or sprinkle wheatgrass seeds upon the earth to thank the harvest gods and goddesses for the bounty they have received. Sprinkle wheat germ, bread crumbs, or seeds upon the earth after a prayer or spell has been answered. Eat any form of wheat to draw steady income.

White

RULER: Moon, Obatala
TYPE: color
MAGICKAL FORM: color, cloth

Use this color for cleansing, purification, healing, protection, and uncrossing rituals. White represents purity and holiness. It is best to wrap in a white towel or bathrobe after a bath to clear away negative energy.

Wild Grapevines

RULER: Dionysus
TYPE: plant
MAGICKAL FORM: woven into wreaths

These vines are popular altar decorations during the fall or harvest season, but they can be worked with throughout the year. In the northeastern United States, the vines are twisted into wreaths and hung above barn doors to protect and energize them. Place any object in a wreath of wild grapevines to consecrate and charge it. The vines will call attention to whatever is placed within its circle.

Willow

RULER: Moon
TYPE: tree
MAGICKAL FORM: branch, bark, leaves

Brooms and wands made of willow branch are a favorite among witches because they help to manipulate or change events. Willow is the best ingredient for shape-shifting or turning a situation around. Carry the leaves in your pocket when you need help adjusting to new situations. Use willow to help you go with the flow.

Wine

RULER: Dionysus
TYPE: alcoholic beverage
MAGICKAL FORM: red, white

By drinking wine, the blood or spirit of Dionysus enters his devotees. So powerful is the elixir of the ancient pagan god of ecstasy that it found its way into important Judeo-Christian rites. Red wine is used in Wiccan circles to make libations to the gods. It is consecrated and then a portion poured off to the earth; coven members share the rest to fill them with blessings. Use *red wine* in love spells and as a substitute for blood. *White wine* is best for purification rites.

Wintergreen, see Mint

Wisteria

RULER: Moon
TYPE: flower
MAGICKAL FORM: oil, petals

To remember your dreams, anoint your third eye or your pillowcase before falling asleep. Anoint pulse points to strengthen ability for astral travel. Burn as incense during psychic work or meditation to receive visions. Add wisteria to love spells to create a dreamy effect.

Witch Grass

RULER: Hecate
TYPE: plant
MAGICKAL FORM: dried

Add some to any formula to increase its power. Offer it to Hecate in a black pot or cauldron along with saltpeter, wormwood, and saffron. Burn the mixture on a dark moon to gain access to her mysteries.

Witch Hazel

RULER: Sun
TYPE: tree
MAGICKAL FORM: astringent, leaves, branch

A wand made of witch hazel quickly opens lines of communication between the priest or priestess and the gods. Brew the leaves into a tea and use it as a body wash when quick purification is needed. A splash of the astringent clears the mind and dispels confusion. Keep some around for focus.

Wolfbane

RULER: Hecate
TYPE: plant
MAGICKAL FORM: bark, leaves

Carry some bark or leaves in a red cloth ouanga bag for courage and fearlessness. Do not let it touch the skin, as it is poisonous. Wolfbane protects those in life-and-death crises. Anyone who risks his life on a daily basis should carry some; so should anyone attempting daredevil-type sports activities such as mountain climbing, flying, skiing steep slopes, and diving.

Woodruff

RULER: Pan
TYPE: plant
MAGICKAL FORM: bark

Also called Master of the Woods, this herb brings success to those who work off the land or seek to commune with nature. Carry some on a journey into the forest to open your sights to fairies and gnomes. Woodruff is also a favorite ingredient to add to gay love spells. It brings frolicking mischief and fun.

Wormwood

RULER: Hecate
TYPE: plant
MAGICKAL FORM: oil, herb

Absinthe is illegal in the United States, but the herb it is derived from is not. Prepare wormwood tea for flying rituals or seep the oil or bark into flying ointments. Its effects are very powerful and should be used with care. Wormwood brings forth hidden mysteries and leads one to the dark side of the moon.

Y

Yam

RULER: Venus
TYPE: vegetable
MAGICKAL FORM: cooked, raw

Yams have incredible drawing power. Push a silver coin into a yam and cook it on a full moon. Eat yams to attract fortune and lucky breaks. Yams are both male and female; the males are oblong and the females are round. Eating the males increases the yang energy; eating the females increases the yin energy. For love spells, roast a male and a female, two females, or two males (depending on your sexual preference) and then combine the two potatoes and eat them with your partner to ensure a long-lasting union. Carve raw sweet potatoes into poppets to attract a mate or bring back an ex-lover. Keep yams on the altar until they grow roots then offer them to the earth with a prayer for love.

Yarrow

RULER: Venus, Kwan-yin
TYPE: plant
MAGICKAL FORM: twigs, leaves

Brew a yarrow tea and drink it to increase your clairvoyant powers. Wash down a room or Ouija board with yarrow to attract friendly spirits. Washing crystals and crystal balls with it brings about a clarity of vision. Yarrow sticks are thrown for I Ching divinations. This is an herb of peace and friendship. It's a great ingredient for attracting friends and family into your life. Yarrow has romantic properties but it is not particularly sexual. It makes a perfect courting ingredient when you want to get to know someone (not in the biblical sense!) first.

Yeast

RULER: Jupiter
TYPE: fungi
MAGICKAL FORM: powder

This is a great ingredient for money drawing, but *do not use it unless you already have a strong financial base*. Since it is very Jupiterian in nature, it makes more of whatever you have. Never use when you have nothing. Use yeast for spells to successfully expand your businesses. It's also great for stock traders and high-stakes gamblers.

Yellow

RULER: Sun
TYPE: color
MAGICKAL FORM: candle, cloth

Use this color for happiness, healing, success, and fame spells. Conception or fertility magick also uses yellow. Offer five yellow fruits or vegetables to a river to protect children. Place yellow flowers in a room to stimulate creative thought.

Yellowdock

RULER: Mercury
TYPE: plant
MAGICKAL FORM: dried

Sprinkle around a place of business to increase sales. Drink the tea for healing and protection.

Yerba Buena

RULER: Jupiter
TYPE: plant
MAGICKAL FORM: dried, oil

Add to gamblers' luck spells to increase your chances of winning. Use on a white candle as a peace offering if you believe you have gotten on the wrong side of the gods. Yerba buena makes them think kindly of you.

Yerba Maté

RULER: Moon
TYPE: herb
MAGICKAL FORM: dried

Yerba maté contains the highest caffeine content of any plant in the world. Drinking it will definitely keep you awake! This herb is believed to improve the physical health and memory, increase stamina, and energize sexual performance. In South American countries, the maté is drunk from a gourd, which is also called a maté. In the United States, it is available in teabag form, although the ritual of drinking from the gourd is said to increase the magickal properties of the maté. Drink to increase concentration, drive away stagnation, and improve general well-being. Use the maté in love spells with dried orange peel added.

Yerba Santa

RULER: Jupiter
TYPE: plant
MAGICKAL FORM: dried, oil

This is an all-round good-works ingredient. Add it to luck and healing recipes for more success. Yerba santa removes obstacles and attracts friendly spirits to your aid.

Yew

RULER: Saturn
TYPE: tree
MAGICKAL FORM: branch, leaves

This is a dark tree ruled by the crone. It is used in spells to raise the dead. Yew is also used in ritual to help make the transition into menopause.

Ylang-Ylang

RULER: Buddha, Kwan-yin
TYPE: flower
MAGICKAL FORM: flower, oil

Wear this fragrance to attract luck in love or business matters. It attracts benevolent spirits and makes wishes come true. Anoint white candles with the oil to solve problems quickly.

Yogurt

RULER: Hathor
TYPE: food
MAGICKAL FORM: milk, soy

Sacred to the Mother Goddess, yogurt is given as an offering to obtain her help and blessing. Eat milk yogurt for comfort, nurturing, and protection. Eat soy yogurt to solve employment matters. Yogurt also brings insight and increases wisdom when eaten on a new moon.

Yohimbe

RULER: Pan
TYPE: herb
MAGICKAL FORM: dried, tincture

Now illegal in the United States, yohimbe has been re-placed by Viagra. It is a lust-inducing herb and used to pro-long penile erections. Mix the herb in wine and share it with lovers to induce wild, passionate sex. Please make sure you have no allergy to product before attempting this.

Yolk

RULER: Sun
TYPE: yellow part of an egg
MAGICKAL FORM: raw

Offer egg yolks to the Sun or eat them raw to gain strength and good health. The yolk is also used to check for psychic attack. If there is a spot of blood in the yellow, there is magick being worked against you; never eat these yolks. To counteract the magick and break the spell, roll nine eggs down your body coun-

terclockwise from head to toe. Do this one at a time. Then place all the eggs in a paper bag and then in a plastic bag. Smash all the eggs in the bag and throw them away at least nine blocks from your house. Follow this ritual with a salt-water and sage bath.

Yoni

RULER: Venus
TYPE: female genitalia
MAGICKAL FORM: candle, statue

Fertility and sex magick uses candles carved into yonis or vaginas. They are also burned for healing illness in the female reproductive system. Keep a yoni statue on the altar to draw down the power of the goddess.

Yucca

RULER: Oya
TYPE: plant
MAGICKAL FORM: flowers, stalk

Offer yucca to the cemetery goddess to overcome fear of death. Women who want to get in touch with their warrior spirit should eat yucca.

Z

Zap

RULER: various
TYPE: spell
MAGICKAL FORM: short candles, fistful of herbs

The magickal zap is a quick-fix spell that is performed in an instant. It can be anything from dusting your palms with a success powder before shaking hands in a business meeting, to using a quick dab of perfumed oil before meeting a lover. Throw a pinch of herbs across a threshold minutes before someone you want to influence walks through the door. Burn short candles when situations call for immediate magickal remedy. The zap teaches the witch that ritual can be inventive and spontaneous.

Zipper

RULER: Mars
TYPE: metal
MAGICKAL FORM: teeth

Quickly pull a zipper up and down five times to get energy moving in a situation. Use zippers to catch someone. Simply write his or her name on a piece of paper and catch the paper in a zipper. Leave it there until you see actual results.

Zucchini

RULER: Jupiter
TYPE: vegetable
MAGICKAL FORM: whole, raw or cooked

For sex magick, use whole raw zucchinis. Place one on the altar and surround with lust herbs to draw a man. To stop a male mate from cheating, carve his name into a zucchini and place in the freezer. (For female lovers use round squash.) Eat cooked zucchini for protection and prosperity.

Magickal Tables

In lieu of an index, which is superfluous in an encyclopedia format, I have prepared the following magickal tables that will help you locate ingredients for the type of spell you wish to work. Check the main section of the book for more specific information about each ingredient.

Magickal Beauty Table

Anchovies	Hibiscus	Olive
Avocado	Honey	Palmarosa
Chervil	Irish moss	Pea
Cypress	Lemon	Raisin
Evening primrose	Mushroom	Sardine

Magickal Communications Table

For promoting good verbal relationships with others as well as communication through writing or artistic expression. Also included are ingredients to improve memory, mental alertness, and intellect.

Arabic gum	Fresia	Rye
Beans	Gotu Kola	Sand
Beech	Hawthorn	Sangria
Beeswax	Honeysuckle	Skunk cabbage
Caraway	Kola nut	Slippery elm
Celery	Lavender	Sodalite
Chestnut	Marshmallow	Styrax
Chickweed	Mastic	Thyme
Cotton	Mint	Topaz
Datura	Moldavite	Turmeric
Dogwood	Newsprint	Woodruff
Elecampane	Pansy	Yarrow
Fennel	Rosemary	

Magickal Creativity Table

Bagel	Horehound	Rain
Barley	Jicama	Rosemary
Basil	Mace	Rye
Beans	Mulberry	Sand
Butterfly	Opal	Sangria
Capers	Orange	Seltzer
Chervil	Papyrus	Snapdragon
Coriander	Pasta	Tansy
Guava	Pickle	Woodruff
Honeysuckle	Plum	

Magickal Employment Table

For finding jobs, protecting businesses, and drawing clients or business.

Beets	Jezebel root	Sesame
Bok choy	Job's tears	Soy
Buckwheat	Lettuce	Swiss chard
Cabbage	Molasses	Tobacco
Cilantro	Oak moss	Tonka
Coffee	Oatmeal	Waffle
Collard greens	Poplar	Wolfbane
Fenugreek	Rattlesnake root	Yellowdock
Flax	Rosehips	Yogurt
Honeysuckle	Seaweed	

Magickal Fertility Table

Barley	Garlic	Oysters
Bloodroot	Guava	Papaya
Celery	Honey	Passion fruit
Corn	Horseradish	Pumpkin
Curry	Horsetail	Sesame
Cyclamen	Hyacinth	Tansy
Egg	Lingam	Tulips
Fennel	Mimosa	Yoni
Fish	Onion	

Magickal Friendship/Social Table

Carob	Kunzite	Rose
Chocolate	Lilac	Rutabaga
Clementine	Maidenhair	Seltzer
Cowslip	Mandarin	Squash
Daffodil	Marigold	Sweetpea
Daisy	Muguet	Tangerine
Dogwood	Narcissus	Tea tree
Elecampane	Nosegay	Tiger's eye
Frangipani	Raspberry	Yarrow
Heather	Rhodochrosite	

Magickal Happiness Table

For curing depression and to foster hope, happiness, and well-being.

Birch	Hyacinth	Raspberry
Bleeding heart	Job's tears	Rhubarb
Carnation	Lamp	Saffron
Chamomile	Maple	Saint-John's-wort
Cherry	Marjoram	Sangria
Chicory	Meadowsweet	Seltzer
Cowslip	Melissa	Sesame
Daffodil	Onyx	Sunflower
Elecampane	Orange	Tangerine
Fig	Peach	Vanilla
Frankincense	Petigrain	Violet
Gold	Pie	Waffle
Grapefruit	Pierogi	Woodruff
Hibiscus	Quince	

Magickal Health Table

For a long life and physical, spiritual, and emotional healing.

Aloe	Frankincense	Patchouli
Angelica	Ginger	Peach
Apple	Ginseng	Pear
Apricot	Gold	Pennyroyal
Aventurine	Hair	Pine
Betony, wood	Heal-all	Pins
Burdock	Hematite	Poppet
Cedar	Jade	Rosehips
Chamomile	Jasper	Sage
Clementine	Juniper	Snakeskin
Cohosh, black	Life everlasting	Sorrel
Coltsfoot	Linden	Sunflower
Comfrey	Lingam	Tea tree
Crystals	Lobelia	Yellowdock
Dandelion	Magnet	Yoni
Dill	Malachite	
Echinacea	Marigold	*For Weight Loss*
Evening primrose	Marshmallow	Anise
Eyebright	Mastic	Celery
Feverfew	Meadowsweet	Poppet
Fig	Olive	Potato
Fir balsam	Oregano	Quartz crystal
Flax	Passion fruit	

Magickal Hexing Table

Ammonia	Ice	Pins
Beets	Jezebel root	Poke
Bittersweet	Knot	Poppet
Cactus	Knotgrass	Snow
Cranberry	Mango	Squill
Datura	Mullein	Sulfur
Hair	Nails	Urine
Henbane	Pepper	Zucchini

Magickal House-Blessing Table

Crab	Iris	Rose of Jericho
Cucumber	Ivy	Rue
Garlic	Lavender	Southernwood
Holly	Mistletoe	Urine
Huckleberry	Pine	

Magickal Love Table

For romancing, seduction, and courtship. These ingredients can be used to attract a new love or deepen an existing one.

Agate	Grapes	Muguet
Anise	Hazel	Mugwort
Apple	Heart	Mullein
Apricot	Heliotrope	Mushroom
Arrowroot	Hemp	Musk
Artichoke	Hickory	Myrhh
Balm of Gilead	Honey	Myrtle
Barley	Honeydew	Nails, Finger- and
Cabbage	Hyacinth	Toe-
Camphor	Jasmine	Nuts
Cardamom	Ketchup	Opal
Carnelian	Key	Opium
Chestnut	Knot	Oregano
Chocolate	Lapus lazuli	Orris
Coconut	Lavender	Pansy
Coltsfoot	Lemon	Paprika
Copper	Linden	Parchment
Coral	Lobelia	Pasta
Cornsilk	Lodestone	Pea
Date	Magnet	Pearl
Deerstongue	Mandrake	Pennies
Dill	Mango	Pesto
Elecampane	Marjoram	Pierogi
Emerald	Marzipan	Pillow
Gardenia	Mistletoe	Pimiento
Gourd	Moonstone	Pins

Plantain
Poppet
Quince
Rain
Roots
Rose
Rose quartz
Ruby
Sandalwood
Sarsaparilla
Silk
Straw, grain
Sugar
Thyme
Tomato
Turnip
Turquoise
Waffle
Woodruff

Yam
Yerba maté
Ylang-ylang

For Soul Mates
Orange
Unicorn root

For Self-Esteem
Camelia
Cherry
Citrine
Clementine
Frankincense
Geranium
Ginkgo
Kunzite
Lily
Makeup

Malachite
Musk
Narcissus
Oak moss
Onyx
Orchid
Orris
Parsley
Patchouli
Petigrain
Pie
Rain
Rose geranium
Ruby
Rue
Sauerkraut
Willow
Wolfbane

Magickal Luck Table

For gambler's luck, general luck, and positive energy.

Acorn	Horsetail	Rue
Agate	Huckleberry	Rum
Angelica	Indian head	Saffron
Bamboo	Irish moss	Sandalwood
Bay	Ivy	Sausage
Beans	Jalup	Seahorse
Beech	Jasper	Seaweed
Bluestone	Khus-khus	Snakeroot
Borage	Lucky hand	Stone
Buckeye	Magnet	Straw, grain
Camphor	Mercury	Sweetgrass
Cinnamon	Mojo beans	Tinfoil
Clover	Moonstone	Tobacco
Coins	Nutmeg	Tonka
Cotton	Nuts	Turkey
Daffodil	Oak moss	Turquoise
Elephant	Opal	Umbrella
Feather	Orange	Waffle
Grains of paradise	Paella	Watermelon
Hand	Parchment	Yerba buena
Henna	Pennies	Yerba santa
Hickory	Pins	Ylang-ylang
Holly	Pizza	
Horseshoe	Roots	

Magickal Power Table

Asparagus	Jasmine	Rutabaga
Borage	Jet	Snakeskin
Burdock	Khus-khus	Spit
Cheese	Lightning	Sword
Cork	Lime	Tears
Cranberry	Makeup	Teeth
Dragonsblood	Molasses	Thorn
Eggplant	Myrtle	Thread
Five-finger	Onion	Thunderbolt
Gardenia	Orange	Vervain
Gold	Orchid	Vetiver
Grapes	Patchouli	Wild grapevines
Hibiscus	Rain	Yew
Iron filings	Roots	Zipper
Jalup	Ruby	

Magickal Protection Table

Aloe	Elder	Lady's slipper
Amber	Elm	Lamb
Arrowroot	Eucalyptus	Larkspur
Artichoke	Eye of newt	Lavender
Asafoetida	Eyes	Lime
Ash	Feather	Lucky hand
Asparagus	Fern	Mace
Bamboo	Feverfew	Mandrake
Bayberry	Fish	Meadowsweet
Bearberry	Five-finger grass	Milk
Betony, wood	Fluorite	Mint
Blueberry	Foxglove	Mirror
Broccoli	Gold	Moonstone
Brussels sprouts	Grains of paradise	Nails, iron
Burdock	Grapefruit	Nightshade
Butter	Hand	Oak
Cactus	Hawthorn	Olive
Cauliflower	Henbane	Palm
Chalk	Henna	Parchment
Citronella	Hickory	Passionflower
Cohosh, black	Holly	Pasta
Corn	Hops	Patchouli
Crab	Horseradish	Pear
Croissant	Huckleberry	Pennyroyal
Cumin	Ice	Pentagram
Curry	Ivy	Peony
Dragonsblood	Jalup	Pepper
Eggplant	Kava kava	Pierogi

Pine
Pins
Plantain
Poppet
Potato
Pretzel
Purselane
Radish
Rice

Roots
Rosehips
Rosemary
Rowan
Rue
Shoes
Skunk cabbage
Snow
Soy

Spit
String
Thistle
Tiger's Eye
Urine
Vetiver
Yellowdock
Yogurt
Zucchini

Magickal Psychic Power Table

For enhancing all forms of clairvoyant work.

Arabic gum
Ash
Bearberry
Belladonna
Borage
Broom
Broom tops
Calamus
Calcite
Cards
Carrot
Datura
Elm
Emerald
Eyebright
Eye of newt
Fluorite
Gardenia
Hawthorn
Hazel
Hellebore

Hemp
Henbane
Henna
Hops
Horehound
Kava kava
Lead
Mercury
Mirror
Moonstone
Morning glory
Mugwort
Mushroom
Nightshade
Olibanum
Peridot
Peyote
Poplar
Poppy
Queen of the
　meadow

Sushi
Topaz
Wormwood

For Dreams
Coral
Dandelion
Elder
Five-finger grass
Mimosa
Nutmeg
Opium
Peony
Periwinkle
Pillow
Poppy
Quartz crystal
Silk
Soy

Magickal Purification and Cleansing Table

Ammonia
Angelica
Baking soda
Bay
Beer
Birch
Carnation
Cascaria
Cassava
Cedar
Chives
Coconut
Copal
Crossroad
Cypress
Date
Devil's shoestring
Doorknob
Egg
Eggplant
Elephant
Eucalyptus
Fir balsam
Flour

Fluorite
Frankincense
Garlic
Hickory
Hydrangea
Juniper
Labdanum
Lamb
Larkspur
Lead
Leeks
Lemon
Lemon verbena
Lily
Lotus
Mayonnaise
Mesquite
Nettle
Palm
Parsley
Patchouli
Pine
Poke
Rain

Rattles
Rose geranium
Rosemary
Rose of Jericho
Rue
Sage
Salt
Saltpeter
Senna
Sesame
Shallot
Sponge
Sulfur
Sweetgrass
Tamarisk
Thyme
Tobacco
Tourmaline
Verbena
Vinegar
Wahoo bark
Witch hazel
Yolk

Magickal Relationship Table

For protecting and nurturing existing relationships and to solve love problems.

Adam and Eve roots	Elder	Rose quartz
Azurite	Ginger	Scullcap
Bedsheets	Hail	Soy
Cedar	Hair	Sunflower
Cranberry	Lime	Vervain
Crocus	Lovage	Vetiver
Cumin	Marigold	Violet
Daffodil	Peach	Watermelon

For Marriage

For attracting a marriage proposal and also to protect and bless a marriage and family.

Honeydew	Orange	Rhubarb
Lady's mantle	Orchid	Rice
Magnolia	Paprika	Rose
Myrtle	Pineapple	Seahorse
Neroli	Poppet	

Magickal Sex Table

Lusty ingredients and aphrodisiacs.

Ambergris	Endive	Papaya
Arugula	Fennel	Patchouli
Asparagus	Frangipani	Pepper
Banana	Garnet	Periwinkle
Basil	Ginseng	Persimmon
Blackberry	Girdle	Radish
Bloodroot	Guarana	Rain
Bristles	Hearts of palm	Shoes
Cactus	Hibiscus	Snail
Cantaloupe	Jezebel root	Strawberry
Cardamon	Juniper	Sushi
Carrot	Kiwi	Tamarind
Catnip	Lemongrass	Tea
Caviar	Lingam	Tobacco
Chocolate	Mint	Vanilla
Civet	Musk	Wahoo bark
Clove	Myrtle	Wine
Coffee	Onion	Yohimbe
Coriander	Orris	Yoni
Damiana	Oysters	Zucchini

Magickal Spiritual Table

For elevating the soul and contacting spirits of the dead.

Acacia	Copal	Olibanum
Amazonite	Corn	Parsley
Ambergris	Dittany of Crete	Petrified wood
Amethyst	Galbanum	Pomegranate
Angelica	Ghee	Pumpkin
Apache tear	Gourd	Rhodochrosite
Aquamarine	Grains of paradise	Rice
Arabic gum	Hemlock	Rose of Jericho
Ash	Hyssop	Rum
Benzoin	Jack-o'-lantern	Spikenard
Beryl	Jet	Sweetgrass
Bread	Key	Tamarisk
Calcite	Lamb	Turkey
Camphor	Lapus lazuli	Verbena
Carnelian	Lily	Vervain
Cedar	Lotus	Wheat
Citron	Marjoram	Wine
Civet	Moldavite	Yew
Clover	Myrhh	Yucca
Coltsfoot	Oleander	

Magickal Stress-Reduction Table

Amethyst	Jasper	Passionflower
Chamomile	Lavender	Pea
Chrysanthemum	Lettuce	Peridot
Cucumber	Mandarin	Potato
Freesia	Melissa	Scullcap
Hematite	Mesquite	Tuberose
Hibiscus	Palmarosa	Valerian

Magickal Success Table

Allspice	Garnet	Orchid
Amber	Guarana	Pancakes
Bamboo	Jalup	Patchouli
Bay	Khus-khus	Pepper
Beech	Kola nut	Roots
Cabbage	Lime	Rose
Chives	Lodestone	Rue
Cilantro	Mace	Sandalwood
Cinnamon	Magnet	Scallion
Citrine	Marzipan	Snail
Citron	Mulberry	Tarragon
Coffee	Mustard	Wasabi
Curry	Neroli	Watercress
Fenugreek	Newsprint	Wolfbane
Frankincense	Nutmeg	Yerba maté
Galangal	Orange	

Magickal Travel Table

For adventure and protection on real and astral journeys.

Ash	Chickweed	Mugwort
Aventurine	Comfrey	Quince
Banana	Heliotrope	Wisteria
Bergamot	Hellebore	
Bloodstone	Hemlock	

Magickal Wealth Table

For prosperity and attracting money.

Alfalfa	Cardamom	Gold
Apple	Cedar	Grains of paradise
Arugula	Cheese	Grapes
Asparagus	Cinnamon	Guava
Bacon	Clove	Herring
Balm of Gilead	Cohosh, black	Honey
Bay	Coins	Irish moss
Bayberry	Corn	Jade
Beans	Cornucopia	Jalup
Bloodstone	Emerald	Jasmine
Borage	Endive	Kiwi
Bread	Fig	Lemon verbena
Brussels sprouts	Fish	Lodestone
Buckwheat	Flax	Magnet
Butter	Flour	Mandrake
Cabbage	Frankincense	Maple

Milk
Moss
Nuts
Oak
Oats
Olive
Orange
Oregano
Paella
Pancakes
Papaya
Paprika
Parchment
Parsnip

Pasta
Patchouli
Pennies
Pesto
Pineapple
Pizza
Plantain
Pomegranate
Pumpkin
Rattlesnake root
Roots
Rose of Jericho
Rue
Saffron

Sandalwood
Sarsaparilla
Sassafras
Snakeroot
Snakeskin
Solomon's seal
Spanish moss
Spinach
Squill
Tea
Wheat
Yam
Yeast
Ylang-ylang

Magickal Wisdom Table

Azalea
Beeswax
Bristles
Crossroad
Cypress
Eggplant
Gold
Grapes
Hazel
Herring

Jade
Jalup
Lamp
Malachite
Maple
Molasses
Myrhh
Nuts
Obsidian
Olive

Owl
Pear
Pepper
Pomegranate
Raisin
Solomon's seal
Witch grass
Yogurt

Bibliography

Budge, E. A. Wallis. *Amulets and Talismans*. New York: University Books, 1968.

Culpeper, Nicholas. *Culpeper's Complete Herbal & English Physician*. Chicago, IL: Meyerbooks, 1990.

Cunningham, Scott. *Encyclopedia of Magical Herbs*. St. Paul, MN: Llewellyn Publications, 1992.

Guirand, Felix, *New Larousse Encyclopedia of Mythology*. Hong Kong: The Hamlyn Publishing Group Ltd., 1972.

Gurudas. *The Spiritual Properties of Herbs*. San Rafael, CA: Cassandra Press, 1988.

Hall, Manly P. *The Secret Teachings of All Ages*. Los Angeles: The Philosophical Research Society, 1977.

Hand, Wayland D., Anna Cassetta, and Sondra B. Theiderman, ed. *Popular Beliefs and Superstitions: A Compendium of American Folklore*. Boston: G. K. Hall, 1981.

Healy, John F., trans. *Pliny the Elder Natural History: A Selection*. London: Penguin, 1991.

Jim, Papa. *Papa Jim Magical Herb Book*. San Antonio, TX: Original Publications, 1985.

Leach, Maria, ed. *Funk & Wagnalls Standard Dictionary of Folklore, Mythology, and Legend*. San Francisco: Harper & Row, 1984.

Lust, John. *The Herb Book*. New York: Bantam, 1974.

Montenegro, Carlos. *Santeria Formulary and Spellbook: A Guide to Nature's Magic*. New York: Original Publications, 1994.

Råtsch, Christian. *Plants of Love: The History of Aphrodisiacs and a Guide to Their Identification and Use*. Berkeley: Ten Speed Press, 1992.

Riva, Anna. *Secrets of Magical Seals*. Los Angeles, CA: International Imports, 1975.

Rose, Donna. *The Magic of Oils*. Hialeah, FL: Mi-World Pub Co., 1978.

Roséan, Lexa. *The Supermarket Sorceress*. New York: St. Martin's Press, 1996.

———. *Zodiac Spells*. New York: St. Martin's Press, 2002.

Slater, Herman, ed. *The Magickal Formulary*. New York: Magickal Childe, 1981.

Tannahill, Raey. *Food in History*. New York: Stein and Day, 1973.

Walker, Barbara. *Women's Encyclopedia of Myths and Secrets*. San Francisco: Harper & Row, 1983.

———. *Women's Encyclopedia of Symbols and Sacred Objects.* San Francisco: HarperCollins, 1988.

Ward, Bernard. *Healing Foods from the Bible.* Boca Raton, FL: Globe Digests, 1994.

Wedeck, Harry, and Wade Baskin. *Dictionary of Pagan Religions.* Secaucus, NJ: Citadel Press, 1973.

Acknowledgments

Patrick Huyghe
Lisa Hagan
Josh Martino
Sarah la Rocca
Madeleine Olnek
Py
Caffe Gelato Dolci
The Morgan Group
Marianna Herro
Enrique Urrutia
Vivian Urrutia
Christopher Kulukundis
Gus Hedrix
Emily